DECORATIVE PAINTING ON

# Glass
# Tile &
# China

Carol Mays

**NORTH LIGHT BOOKS**

CINCINNATI, OH

www.artistsnetwork.com

## About the Author

Carol Mays is a decorative painter, designer and teacher. She is the author of eight books on decorative painting and has created numerous pattern packets on both decorative and glass painting. She and her husband David run their business called A Couple of Ideas in Tulsa, Oklahoma. Her Web site is www.ACoupleofIdeas.com.

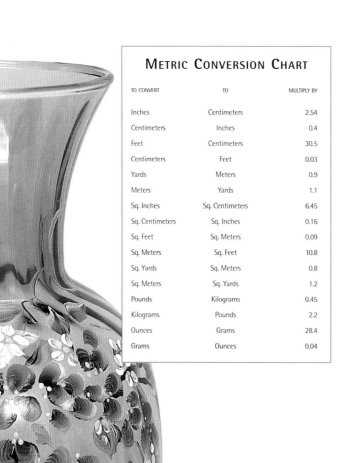

### METRIC CONVERSION CHART

| TO CONVERT | TO | MULTIPLY BY |
|---|---|---|
| Inches | Centimeters | 2.54 |
| Centimeters | Inches | 0.4 |
| Feet | Centimeters | 30.5 |
| Centimeters | Feet | 0.03 |
| Yards | Meters | 0.9 |
| Meters | Yards | 1.1 |
| Sq. Inches | Sq. Centimeters | 6.45 |
| Sq. Centimeters | Sq. Inches | 0.16 |
| Sq. Feet | Sq. Meters | 0.09 |
| Sq. Meters | Sq. Feet | 10.8 |
| Sq. Yards | Sq. Meters | 0.8 |
| Sq. Meters | Sq. Yards | 1.2 |
| Pounds | Kilograms | 0.45 |
| Kilograms | Pounds | 2.2 |
| Ounces | Grams | 28.4 |
| Grams | Ounces | 0.04 |

Other fine North Light Books are available from your local bookstore or art supply store or direct from the publisher.

06  05  04  03  02     5  4  3  2  1

**Library of Congress Cataloging-in-Publication Data**

Mays, Carol.
    Decorative painting on glass, tile, and china / Carol Mays.
       p.cm.
    Includes index.
    ISBN 1-58180-156-4
    1. Glass painting and staining. 2. China painting. I. Title.

TT298 .M38 2002
745.7`23--dc21

                                           2001052141

Editor: Gina Rath

Production Coordinator: Mark Griffin

Designer: Joanna Detz

Photographers: Christine Polomsky and Tim Grondin

## Dedication

This book is dedicated with love to my two daughters, Keli and Kim, and to my daughter-in-law, Renee. Their love for painted glass and for me have given me the enthusiasm and inspiration to pursue new and innovative ideas on glass.

As this book goes to press, my life has been wonderfully enriched by the birth of my first granddaughter, Caroline Elizabeth Mays. My three adorable grandsons, Zachary and Joshua Hassman and Alex Mays, welcome her with open arms into our loving family.

## Acknowledgments

A Special Thanks goes to my best friend, who also happens to be my husband of 41 years. He makes my life so fun and easy. His incredible wisdom and understanding helped make the many months of developing this book amazingly stress-free and rewarding.

I also want to thank Kathy Kipp, Gina Rath and Christine Polomsky, my new friends at North Light Books. Their expertise and encouragement has helped my dream come true.

# Table of Contents

# Introduction

Making this book was a challenge that I eagerly accepted. Glass painting brings so much joy to my life, and I welcome the opportunity to share it with others. It is my wish that you will experiment with the patterns and ideas presented in this book and that they will inspire you to experiment with ideas of your own.

Painting on glass, tile and china can be either an exciting and gratifying experience or, without correct information and the proper supplies, possibly a very frustrating undertaking. I have found that with just a few adjustments of your tools and some additional ideas and techniques, you can eliminate frustration and replace it with glass painting fun!

Please do not try to achieve the controlled and precise realistic painting that you may be accustomed to achieving on other surfaces. Today's glass painting style is carefree, loose and forgiving. It also shows imagination and pizzazz and doesn't expect technical perfection. This is not a license to get sloppy, however; but do have fun and let it show in your work!

Ten years ago when I first started painting on glass, it was very difficult to find surfaces to decorate.

I had to search high and low for white porcelain dishes and accessories that would be suitable for me to paint. But now, it is so exciting to walk into a craft or department store or discount center and see the amazing displays of unpainted glassware available to choose from. I take full advantage of that availability. All of the glass, tile and china pieces in this book were purchased from these types of stores. If you cannot find the identical piece of glass that I have used in this book, it's easy to find a similar piece and adjust the pattern to fit your selection. I hope you will enjoy painting on the pieces I have selected and that you will also find new and exciting pieces of glassware to use for your own designs in the future.

The information in this book was compiled through many hours of experiments that resulted in both failures and successes. I always learn more from an experiment that did not work because I can figure out what went wrong and then work on ways to make it better. I share this information with you, hoping you'll use the ideas you like, discard the ideas you don't like, and never stop experimenting on your own. And when you find something wonderful—call me!

CHAPTER ONE

# Materials

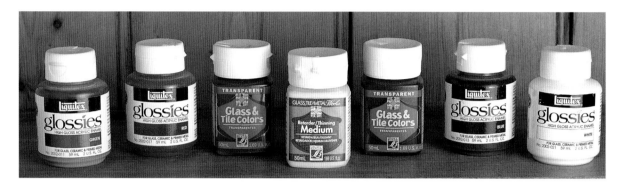

## Acrylic Enamels for Glass

Many different brands of glass paint are on the market. Each brand has its own specific instructions that are required to ensure the durability of the paint when applied to glass and slick surfaces. It is imperative that you refer to these instructions before starting any project and choose the method most suitable for you. Most brands need to be baked in the home oven; but some need special applications of conditioners and topcoats and specific curing times before the glassware can be used. Baking time and temperature varies between brands, so be diligent about following the specific directions for each brand. This will ensure the durability and permanency of the finished painted glassware.

## Brand Requirements

• **Liquitex Glossies** Painted glass must be allowed to dry overnight to cure, then baked at 325° for 45 minutes.
• **Plaid FolkArt Gloss** Painted glass must be allowed to dry overnight to cure, then baked at 325° for 10 minutes.
• **DecoArt Gloss** Permanent when allowed to cure for 7 days after painting is dry. More durable and scratch-resistant if baked in a home oven at 325° for 30 minutes.
• **Lefranc & Bourgeois Glass & Tile** Must be baked at 300° for 30 minutes.
• **Delta Perm Enamel** Brush on Delta's Surface Conditioner and let dry. Apply paint and let dry 1 hour. Top coat with Delta's Clear Gloss or Satin Glaze—two coats—letting it dry 1 hour between coats. Let dry for 10 days before washing.

The projects in this book were painted using Liquitex Glossies, with the exception of the Stained Glass Bottle project on which I used Lefranc & Bourgeois Glass & Tile Paint. Therefore, the color instructions are given using the Liquitex brand. Some colors of other brands may be more transparent than the Liquitex Glossies and may need two coats of paint to cover. The paint must be completely dry before you reapply.

The techniques of painting for all brands of paint will be similar; it is just the specific process for making the paint permanent that will vary. Be sure to check the instructions for each particular brand of paint to ensure your success.

# Brushes

Many people become frustrated when they try to paint on glass because of the streaky and uneven coverage, which results in a messy look. This is easily remedied by using the correct brush.

After years of personally experimenting with many different brands of paint and brushes, I can assure you that the streaky and messy appearance is not the fault of the paint brand. It is more likely caused by the type of brush being used.

It is imperative that you use the right kind of brushes when painting on glass. The biggest mistake most first-time glass painters make is using the same kind of synthetic brushes they use for their other acrylic painting.

Painting on glass is different than painting on other surfaces like wood or metal. The hard slick surface of the glass will reject the springiness of synthetic brush bristles and will cause irregular paint coverage, which can be disappointing and unacceptable.

I have found that extremely soft brushes (some of which are totally useless when painting other surfaces) will provide excellent results on glass. Soft-bristled brushes will lay the paint onto the glass and will not push or spring away from the slick surface, resulting in smooth, complete coverage.

I never quit experimenting and am constantly finding soft and wonderful brushes for glass painting. I have listed for you my favorite tools that make glass painting easier and more fun for me.

## Soft Brushes

Soft brushes are used for laying the paint on the glass. The following are my favorites.
- **White Taklon brushes made by Royal Brush** have very soft synthetic hairs, and I use them extensively throughout this book. I use the following series:
   Series no. 150 Shader in various sizes 2 through 8.
   Series no. 159 Short Shader in sizes 0 through 6.
   Series no. 179 Cats Tongue (filbert) in sizes 2 and 4.
   Series no. 599 Liner in sizes 5/0, 0, 1, and 2.
- **Lefranc & Bourgeois Glass & Tile Brushes Set** (includes a shader and a round).
- **Royal Natural Hair Round Brush Set No. 225** This set contains about five round brushes that are ideal for painting on glass. I use the nos. 1, 3 and 5 in this book.

- **Royal/Langnickel Series 5005, sizes 8, 10 and 12** This is one of my most important brushes. No other company makes a similar brush as far as I know. This is a stubby but soft brush that is useful for many glass-painting techniques. I use it for almost all drybrushing and also for dabbing in highlights and shadows when I am painting in the reverse technique.
- **Optional brushes to consider** are cheap (inexpensive) natural hair or sable brushes. Do not buy the expensive sable brushes as they have too much spring and the acrylic enamel paint is just too hard on them. It is not necessary to have such fine brushes for glass painting.

Another of my favorite brushes is a lipstick brush made from natural hairs that I received as a sample at a makeup party. I have tried other inexpensive sable lipstick brushes, and they seem to work equally well. You can use this brush in place of the no. 4 flat shader that I list in many of my projects. Experiment with various natural hair brushes and find the ones most suitable for you. You should see an amazing difference in control and coverage when you find just the right brush.

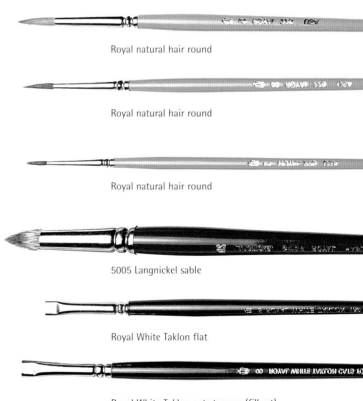

Royal natural hair round

Royal natural hair round

Royal natural hair round

5005 Langnickel sable

Royal White Taklon flat

Royal White Taklon cats tongue (filbert)

## Miscellaneous Supplies

• **Q-tips** These are great for cleaning up boo-boos. Just dip the tightened tip in a tad of rubbing alcohol and all of your mistakes will vanish! I remove about half of the cotton from the end of the tip, then roll it in my fingers to tighten the remaining cotton to the stick, then carefully remove the mistake. Off-brand swabs do not work as well for me. I also use Q-tips to paint dots and small flower petals.

• **Wax-free transfer paper** Sally's by Saral is the brand I prefer for transferring patterns onto glass surfaces.

• **Miracle Sponge** You can cut the dry, flat Miracle Sponge into any shape, place it in water and watch it expand! Then the shape can be used to sponge paint onto the glassware.

• **Rubbing alcohol** I use rubbing alcohol for cleaning up mistakes and for cleaning the glass before painting.

• **Lintless paper towels** I prefer Job Squad or Viva. Cheap paper towels work fine for other painting, but when painting on glass, I need soft towels that leave no lint.

• **Scotch Magic Tape** I use this for taping the pattern or design onto the glass.

• **Permanent pen** I use a permanent ink pen (such as Sakura Identi-pen) with a tiny point for tracing the pattern onto the reverse side of a glass surface.

• **Toothpicks** Toothpicks are great for making tiny dots. You can also outline with a little thinned paint on the end of a toothpick. I lightly sand the sharp tip off with an emery board so it is still pointed but dulled a bit. I also make great looking tiny flowers by making a dot and then slightly pulling to form a petal. This creates a very sophisticated looking little flower.

## Glassware Preparation

No brand of paint will be permanent even when baked in the oven if you do not properly prepare the glassware ahead of time. This is the most critical step to successfully painting on glassware and must be faithfully performed. The majority of failures result because of poor or no preparation.

Wash the glassware in warm sudsy water to remove all traces of oil and dirt. Rinse thoroughly and allow to dry. To remove any soap residue use lintless paper towels and wipe the surface with rubbing alcohol or a 1:1 vinegar-and-water mixture. While painting the glassware, do not touch the area to be painted with your fingers. Even if they are scrupulously clean, your hands contain oils, which will form a barrier between the paint and the glass. This will affect adhesion. Handle the glassware very carefully and try to touch it only in the places where no paint will be applied.

## Baking in the Oven

Many painters balk at the idea of baking painted glassware in a home oven. However, with Liquitex and certain other brands of glass paint, this makes them more permanent. I personally do not find it troublesome to bake painted glass items in my oven.

I have found that the items can either be placed on a baking sheet or directly on the oven rack with no apparent danger. I have baked all thicknesses of glass to experiment with the safety of the baking process, and I have never had a piece of glass break in the oven. Even the most fragile glass makes it through the baking process very successfully.

The items should be placed in a cool oven so the glass is allowed to heat gradually until it reaches the desired temperature. A slight odor is emitted from the oven during the baking process, but it is not annoying to me. The odor is not toxic, but if it is offensive to you, I suggest wearing a breathing mask or pick that time to do some gardening or sunbathing. As my dear husband will attest, I have had a lot worse odors coming from my oven!

## Baking a Stack of Glassware

Because I often have entire sets of glass dishes to bake, I have experimented and discovered the following time-saving technique. When I am baking a set of plates, I arrange copper pennies in stacks of four and place three or four stacks equally distributed on one plate. I then place another plate on top of these stacks of pennies, then stack more pennies, then add another plate, and so on as shown above. I usually bake about eight plates per stack. Bowls can be stacked in a similar manner.

When stacking glassware in this manner, I extend the baking time by five minutes. I have never broken any dishes using this method, and the pennies do not get too hot to cause any problems. Always turn off the oven and let the dishes cool before taking them out of the oven to prevent getting burned.

## Using a Dishwasher

Many brands of paint boast that they are dishwasher safe when the proper procedures are used in the paint application process, and my own experience has confirmed this claim. However, I personally consider all of my painted glassware as highly treasured as fine china, so I recommend hand washing only.

Because of today's high-powered dishwashers and dishwashing products that contain abrasives and bleach, I do not want to gamble on even the slightest color change or fading of my painted items. On all of my pieces that I sell, I attach a fancy tag stating that they should be treated just like fine china and should be hand washed only.

## Safe to Use?

Even though most of the glass paints on the market are nontoxic, it is not recommended that you paint on the surfaces that will come in contact with food. This puzzled me as I knew it was safe to ingest the paint itself—so why not eat from a painted plate? The reason is, when cutting food on a plate, there is a chance that the paint could be pierced with a sharp edge and cause an indentation. Even though this indentation may not be visible to the human eye, it could form a trap for bacteria to hide (similar to a crack in a plate) and thus the danger. This is the reason the paint manufacturers must say that paint should not be used on surfaces that will come in contact with food.

This brings up a special challenge when designing painted glassware. Clear glass plates must be painted in reverse (see next page, Reverse Glass Painting). That means the design is seen on the surface but the painting is actually on the underside and solid plates should be painted on the rim only.

## Reverse Glass Painting

Because you will be looking through the glass to see the design, you will have to paint everything in reverse order, starting with the highlights and embellishments and lastly filling in the object.

The steps you would normally do first will have to be done last, which can become confusing. For example, any final linework or curlicues that overlap onto the main part of the design should be painted in first so they will show when looking through the front of the glass.

Also, the colors will not be as vivid when looking through the glass as they are when painted on the front, but when it's finished, the effect is still very pleasing.

As you can see, a reverse-painted design must be well planned, as it is extremely disappointing to find out after finishing that you have left out a step. But if you follow the easy, step-by-step instructions in this book, you will soon get the hang of it, and you will be designing your own reverse-painted plates before you know it!

## Strokework

Now is the time to perfect your strokework. Or, it could be time to go and kiss your strokework teacher who insisted that you learn and practice the basics of beautiful strokework!

Nothing makes glass painting easier, faster and more fun than being able to confidently execute strokework flowers, fruits and leaves on glass. When doing a strokework design using the reverse painting technique, take care not to overlap the strokes. Each stroke must have its own space or the design will be distorted and unpleasant. Also, take care when double loading your brush; keep the dark edge dark and the light edge sharp and light and allow the colors to fade into each other in the middle of the brush.

## Transferring the Pattern

I have had very good luck simply tracing my pattern on using wax-free Sally's Graphite Transfer Paper by Saral. I use the gray on clear glass and the white or yellow Saral on colored glass.

Tape the pattern face down to the opposite side of the glass so it shows through to the side you are painting on.

Another option is to tape the pattern face down onto the side that you will be painting on so that it shows through to the other side. Then trace the major outlines of the pattern with a permanent pen. These lines will not be on the side that you are painting on but will actually show through to the other side.

The advantage of this is that it is a little easier to paint from the outlines than from a paper pattern. When all the painting is complete, use rubbing alcohol on a Q-tip or lint-free paper towel to remove the inked lines from the glass.

You can also draw patterns freehand using a china marking pencil.

## Helpful Tips

• Glass paint dries fast on the palette but slow on glass. It always looks shiny so it is hard to tell by looking if it is dry or not. The paint is dry when it is no longer tacky to the touch. Remember: have patience!
• You cannot use a wet palette with this paint as it changes the consistency of the paint.
• Make sure you wipe all of the water out of your brush on a paper towel before you reload it with paint.
• When you load your brush, push hard and fill the brush full of paint.
• Most of all, relax and have fun!

# CHAPTER TWO

# Techniques

## Brush Loading Techniques

Loading the brush with paint means more than sticking the brush into paint and then applying the paint to your surface. You must have a proper brush load with enough paint worked into the brush to carry it nicely over the surface without leaving ridges. Ridges result when the outside surface of your brush contains too much paint that has not been worked into the hairs.

Dip the bristles of the brush into a puddle of paint. Apply pressure as you stroke through the side of the paint. Keep stroking and applying pressure on the palette (pushing down on the hairs as shown) so you can force the paint into the bristles and not just let it remain on the outside of the bristles. When I say fully loaded it does not mean that the brush will be oozing with paint. It just means that the bristles have been filled with paint all the way through (but not all the way up to the metal ferrule)

then blended so there are no heavy globs of paint on the outside edges.

This seems so simple, but without proper brush loading, it is very hard to achieve beautiful brushstrokes and nice smooth basecoating.

**Double Loading Your Brush** First properly load your brush in the basecoat color as instructed above. Then tip one corner into the highlight color and blend the two colors together on the palette, stroking in the very same area. Sometimes I ever-so-lightly creep my brush bristles from side to side to help the colors blend together without a line.

**Triple Loading Your Brush** Properly load the brush in the medium color, then tip one corner into the light color and the other corner into the dark color. Blend as you did for the double-loaded brush.

## Brush Loading Techniques continued

**Loading Your Stippling Brush** Load your brush with the first color, then hold the brush horizontally as you slide the edge of the bristles through the second color.

Pounce on the paint. The stippler is mainly used to make flower centers.

## Basecoating

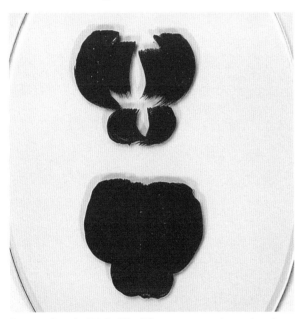

**Basecoating the Wrong Way** Using too small of a brush and too much paint can result in ridges.

**Basecoating the Right Way** There are many times when I will tell you to basecoat making shape-following strokes. Always use the largest brush you can for basecoating.
Top: the stroke direction on a strawberry.
Bottom: the completed strawberry (one coat).

# Floating and Highlighting

Liquitex Glossies paint may be mixed with water without compromising the binder or losing adhesion. A ratio of 20% water to 80% paint is a safe formula. It is the only paint brand that I'm familiar with that can be floated using water. Other brands of paint provide a thinning medium to be used for floating color and for linework. If you are using another brand of paint, you must use the thinning medium for that particular brand. Do not mix brands of medium and paint as it may adversely affect the results.

**Properly Loaded Brush** Dip the brush into the paint or medium. Press the side of the brush into the paint and blend on your palette to distribute the paint. The paint should be dark on one edge and fade away before it gets to the other side of the brush. (Remember to press the brush to push the paint into the bristles.)

**Straight Float** Once you have the brush properly loaded you are ready to float the color. This is how it will look.

**Wiggle Float** You can use the wiggle float to create pleats in flowers and veins next to flower centers. Hold the brush on the chisel edge with the paint pointing toward the center of the flower. Press firmly as you apply a zigzag float to the petal. The dark will touch the center of the flower and fade away toward the outside of the petal.

# Dry Brush Highlighting

The Royal/Langnickel Sable 5005 brush is the only one I prefer to use for this technique. Load the brush very sparingly with paint, then wipe it on a paper towel to remove the excess paint.

**First Highlight** Drybrush the first highlight with yellow. Skim the surface with a very light touch using the Langnickel brush.

**Final Highlight** For a final highlight, drybrush white into the middle.

# Basic Brushstrokes

**Comma Stroke** Press down to begin the fat part of the stroke.

Allow the brush to lift up to a point to finish.

**Cradled Comma Stroke** To make a cradled comma stroke, start the second comma stroke where the first one starts to thin; then follow the curve and end at approximately the same point. The two comma strokes should not touch each other; they should have a small space separating them.

**S-Stroke** Begin the S-stroke on the chisel edge of a flat or the point of a round brush; slide, turn, then press down to form the middle of the stroke.

Continue and lift back up to the chisel edge or point to end the stroke.

**Ribbon Stroke** Start on the chisel edge of your brush, slide as you press down to form a wide middle. Allow the brush to lift back up to the chisel edge as you near the end of the stroke. End with a thin line. (Note: A ribbon stroke can also be done with a round brush. Start on the point of the brush and drag as you press the brush down to form a wide middle, dragging as you release pressure to return to the point of the brush.)

**Curlicues** Use a liner brush and paint thinned with either water or thinning medium (depending on your paint brand). It is easier to make curlicues if you have some image in mind as you execute the stroke. Think of making a few *e*'s, then swing the brush around in a reverse motion and make some *m*'s You will achieve easy vine-like curlicues.

# Leaf Strokes Using Your Filbert Brush

**One-Stroke Leaf** Using your filbert brush, press down on the bristles.

Slide and lift up to the point.

**Two-Stroke Leaf** To form a larger two-stroke leaf, simply combine two one-stroke leaves.

# Leaf Strokes Using Your Flat Brush

The starting position for the leaf stroke is very important. Using a flat brush, paint a V shape for the starting position of the leaf.

Each stroke begins with the chisel edge of your brush on the V starting position. Place your brush on one side of the V and stroke in the first half of the leaf by pushing the brush, then lifting up to a point.

Turn your work to make the second half of the leaf. Make sure the chisel edge is in position on the other side of the V shape and stroke in the second half of the leaf in the same manner.

# Creating Flowers and Petals

## Daisy Petals

Both daisy petals shown here are created using the same stroke. This is simply a press-and-pull stroke, but by turning your filbert brush and using either the flat edge or chisel edge of the brush, you can vary the look of the petals.

**Flat Edge**

**Chisel Edge**

**Filler Flowers (above left)** Using a no. 2 short flat brush, start on the chisel edge, press down and swivel. Using a brush with shorter hairs makes it easier to swivel and stop without an overswing. The size of the brush determines the petal size, as the only motion is a swirl. By changing the size of your brush you will vary the size of your blossom.

**Alternate Filler Flowers (above right)** Double load your no. 2 filbert; keep the second color on the tip. Start on the chisel edge; press, then lift to form a single blossom. Do not pull or drag the brush but lift directly up.

**Dip-Dots (left)** To make dip-dots, make sure your paint is fresh and in a nice round puddle on your palette. Dip a toothpick into the paint and touch onto the desired area. Wipe the toothpick often to remove excess paint. You can also use the following tools to make dip-dots of any size:
• Large dots with end of a brush handle
• Smaller dots with the sanded point of a toothpick
• Smallest dots with the sharp point of a new toothpick

# Helpful Hints

**Correcting Mistakes** Use rubbing alcohol on a Q-tip to clean up a small mistake or to sharpen an edge. You can remove some of the cotton from the end of the Q-tip to have more control of the cleanup.

**Wound** If you do not allow the paint to dry thoroughly between each coat, the first coat will peel away from the glass, creating a "wound." A wound cannot be covered up as it just gets worse with each application of color. You must remove the entire area completely with rubbing alcohol and start over.

**Pattern Inside a Glass** When painting a glass you want the pattern to stay close against the glass. Here's a helpful tip that I use. Trim the pattern close to the design. Bend the pattern into the inside of the glass and secure with Scotch Magic Tape. Stuff a paper towel into the glass to push the pattern snugly against the side of glass.

# Sponge Preparation

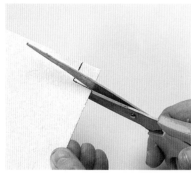

With scissors or a craft knife, cut a Miracle Sponge into the desired shape for the project.

Drop the sponge into clean water.

Make sure all the moisture is squeezed out before adding paint. I squeeze the sponge between paper towels to remove any remaining moisture.

# *Children's*
# Party Plates

Y ou can buy clear glass plates and mugs at any crafts store, discount store, home store or retail department store. My grandchildren are going to enjoy using these special party plates, and what fun I will have celebrating along with them!

This project is a great introduction to the reverse glass painting method described in chapter one. It's a simple project and the steps are clear and easy to follow. As I mentioned earlier, when you're doing reverse painting, just think backwards!

## Paint = Liquitex Glossies

Purple

Pink

Bright Blue

Yellow

Red

Pine Green

Green

Black

Purple + White (1:1)

Pink + Red (3:1)

White + Green (4:1)

White

Orange

## Materials

### ROYAL BRUSHES

▷ Series 159, no. 4 White Taklon flat

▷ Series 225, no. 5 sable round

▷ Series 179, no. 2
White Taklon cats tongue (filbert)

▷ Series 599, no. 0 and no. 1 White Taklon liners, or Series 225, no. 0 and no. 1 sable rounds

▷ Series 5005, no. 14 Langnickel sable

### ADDITIONAL SUPPLIES

▷ rubbing alcohol

▷ paper towels

▷ permanent fine-point pen

▷ Scotch Magic Tape

▷ toothpicks

▷ Q-tips

▷ hair dryer

### SURFACE

▷ Clear glass dessert plates from any craft, hobby or home supply store.

These patterns may be hand-traced or photocopied for personal use only. Enlarge at 200%, then again at 111% to bring them up to full size.

# First Steps

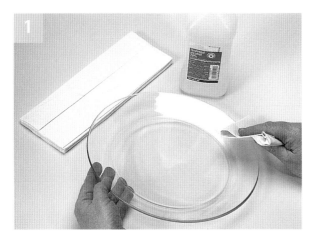

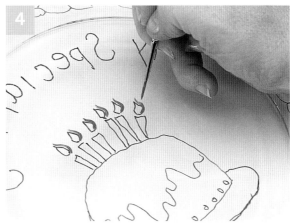

**1** Clean the glass surface thoroughly with rubbing alcohol and a lint-free paper towel.

**2** Tape the pattern to the back of the plate, and with your permanent pen trace the pattern onto the front of the plate. You will be doing reverse glass painting, so although the pattern is traced onto the front of the plate, you'll be painting on the reverse, or back of the plate. Remove the taped pattern and turn the plate over to paint on the back of the plate. The advantage of tracing the design onto the front and looking through the plate while you paint is that you can check your work as you paint without having to untape and lift the pattern to view your painting.

**3** Since it is necessary to handle the edges of the plate while painting the bottom, I recommend waiting until you are completely finished painting the plate bottom before you prepare and apply the pattern to the rim of the plate. When you do apply the border pattern, tape

the design onto the top (front) of the plate. Then turn the plate over and trace the pattern onto the back of the plate rim. You will then paint the front.

**4** In reverse glass painting you must first paint what shows through to the front of the glass. With this project you will simply be filling in between the lines. Starting with your no. 0 liner and Orange, outline the right side of the candle flames. Make sure you are painting on the back of the plate.

---

## Hint

With glass be carefree and happy in your work. It does not need to be perfect.

# Outlining

 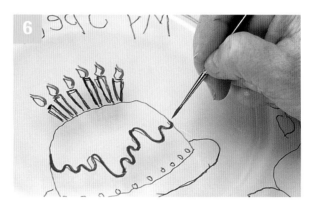

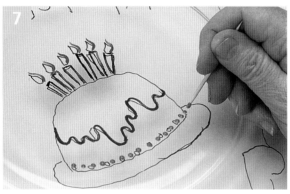 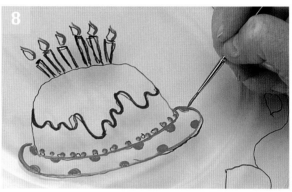

**5** Still using your no. 0 liner, outline the candles with Purple.

**6** With the same brush, outline the icing with Red.

**7** Using a dulled (see page 10) wooden toothpick, dot Pink along the bottom of the icing.

**8** Use Bright Blue and your no. 0 liner to outline the cakeplate and to color in the blue polka dots on the plate.

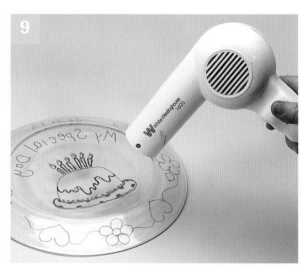

**9** Dry the paint with a hair dryer—this step must be thoroughly dry before you can go on to the next step.

## Hint

With glass painting you must have patience. Let the paint dry thoroughly between coats or the second coat of paint will cause the first coat to pull off.

# Filling In

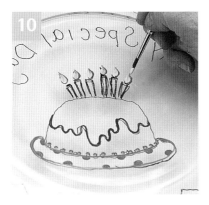  

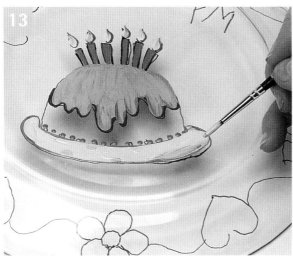 

**10** For the candle flames, use your no. 1 liner with Yellow mixed with just a touch of White. (See the hint at the bottom of this page.)

**11** Using the same brush, fill in the candles with Purple and White (1:1) mixed to a light purple.

**12** Using your no. 5 round, mix Pink and Red (3:1). Leave the paint a little bit streaky; don't worry about mixing it thoroughly. I usually do not use my brush to mix paint, but because a variation in color is desired for the icing, I have made an exception here. Paint in the icing using this mix. Flatten the brush as much as possible for good coverage. This icing section will take two coats. Dry thoroughly between coats.

**13** Mix White and Green (4:1) to make a light green. Using your no. 5 round, fill in the cake plate. Cover over the dots that you have already painted on the plate. You may need a second coat.

**14** This is how the plate will look at this point from the front (the side you are not painting on).

---

## Hint

Yellow is a very transparent color. A touch of White paint makes it more opaque without changing the color intensity. I always add White to my Yellow (1:6).

# Words and Outer Rim

**15** Using your no. 5 round and White, fill in the white icing over the entire cake, even over the pink icing. If there are any streaks left in the pink icing, the White will cover over this. If you get out of line, use your Q-tip to make corrections.

**16** Outline the words with your no. 0 liner and Purple. You can mix this with a tiny bit of water if you are using Liquitex paints. If you are using any other brand, use their thinning medium. If you're right-handed start on the left, and if you're left-handed start on the right. This keeps your hand from getting into the paint.

Use the end of your liner brush handle to apply the dots with fresh Purple paint. This will make larger dots than the toothpick will.

**17** Using Pink and your no. 1 liner, outline the lifeline (the squiggly pink line around the cake). Whenever you are running out of paint, stop and make two dots; reload your brush, then continue on with the pink lifeline.

I call these two dots "taking a breath between the life-lines." This way you don't have to try and connect the lines when you run out of paint on your brush. Besides, it looks happy and fun to have these breaks in the lifeline.

**18** Use the brush handle to apply White dots around the cake. Continue with light green dots around the lifeline in the same manner. (This green is the same 4:1 Green and White mixture that you used on the plate earlier.)

It is now time to paint on the outer rim of the front of the plate. You may need to apply the rest of your pattern at this point. Use your no. 4 flat with a mixture of Purple and White (1:1) to fill in the hearts. Fill in the ribbon using Pink with just a touch of White. Dry thoroughly at this point. When dry, apply a second coat to both the hearts and the ribbon.

# Ribbons and Hearts

**19** Double load your no. 2 filbert brush with a light purple mix of Purple and White (1:10) and Purple. Keep the darker purple side of the brush turned toward the outside edge of the heart.

**20** Using your no. 4 flat, double load Pink and Red. Keep the darker Red paint toward the inside of the knot and toward the tail of the bow.

**21** Float a little White on the outside edges. Load your brush with water or thinning medium and highlight the outside edges and the tail of the bow.

**22** Dot the outside edges of the hearts with a dulled toothpick and White. Be very careful to space the dots so they are not touching (if they touch they will run together). Also make three-dot flowers in the heart. These are flowers made with three purple dots and one White dot in the center. Randomly place White dots throughout the rest of the heart and throughout the ribbon.

## Hint

Don't try to clean up the edges if your edges look rough. It's okay if it isn't perfect. You will be adding dots and they will cover up any imperfections.

# Flowers and Leaves

**23** Load your no. 4 flat with Bright Blue and dip the tip into White.

**24** Start on the outside edge of the petal and stroke toward the middle, two strokes per petal. It is important to reload after each petal. Dry thoroughly. You should need only one coat. Any light that might show through just makes it look shaded.

**25** Load your no. 14 sable with Yellow, touch it into White, then side load with a little bit of Orange on one edge. Stipple on your palette to make sure the Orange is only on one edge. Keep the Orange turned toward the outside edge of your plate and just dab this into the center of your flowers. Be careful that the Orange doesn't overpower the Yellow.

**26** Using your no. 2 filbert and the Green and White mixture, paint the leaves using a two-stroke leaf stroke. Begin near the flower petals and stroke out.

**27** With the same Green and White mixture and your no. 0 liner, paint the vine.

**28** With a pointed toothpick, dot White around all the flowers and the leaves. Add a few random dots on the blue flower petals. Dot Pine Green through the center of the leaves. Remember not to let the dots touch each other.

  Apply Black dots to the center of the flowers in a zigzag pattern. Allow these dots to look loose and free.

# Final Steps

**29** To finish up you need to remove the pattern from your plate. (Remember, the pattern is on the opposite side from where you painted.) Use rubbing alcohol and a paper towel to carefully remove any of the inked pattern. Be especially careful not to touch any of the paint on the outer rim with the alcohol. Bake according to your paint manufacturer's instructions. When baking reverse-painted glass, turn the plate so the painted area is facing up; this allows the heat to circulate.

## Instructions for Balloon Plate

All of this design is painted on the back of the plate. Prepare the glass and trace on the pattern the same as for the Special Day plate. Paint the design in this order:

**1** Paint all the strings using Gold and your no. 0 liner. Make sure you place the strings around the neck of each balloon. Thin the paint just enough so that it flows smoothly. Let dry. Lightly outline the Gold strings with Black. Outline all of the balloons on one side of the balloon, some on the left and some on the right. Do not go all the way around the balloon with the black line, but let it disappear as you lift up the brush.

**2** Paint highlights in all the balloons using White. (The highlight is a dot with a line underneath.)

**3** Paint the balloons using the photo as a guide for the colors. Some of the colors may take two coats.

**4** The words, Happy Birthday, are lined in Blue. Place dots at the ends of each letter with your brush end.

**5** Paint the confetti using all the colors that were used on the balloons. Use the chisel edge of your no. 2 filbert and just touch it to the surface; then lift to make small confetti shapes. You do

not want these to look like dip dots. Use the liner brush to make curly lines to represent confetti tape.

Allow the paint to dry and bake the plate according to the instructions on the paint bottle.

# *Glass*

# Salad Bowl

This is the ideal project for gift giving because it is very inexpensive, it paints up fast and easy and it is bright and colorful. If you can find a set of four smaller glass bowls, you can paint them up at the same time you're working on the large bowl.

I have had to purchase two more sets of bowls because both my daughters have laid claim to this project.

For ease of painting, try placing the large bowl on a turntable or a lazy Susan, so you don't tip the bowl over and cause wet paint to smear.

## Materials

### ROYAL BRUSHES

▶ Series 4020, no. 8 Snow White filbert

▶ Series 179, no. 2 White Taklon cats tongue (filbert)

▶ Series 225, no. 5 sable round

▶ Series 159, no. 4 White Taklon flat

▶ Series 5005, no. 14 Langnickel sable

### ADDITIONAL SUPPLIES

▶ Miracle Sponge

▶ rubbing alcohol

▶ paper towels

▶ Scotch Magic Tape

▶ toothpicks

▶ hair dryer

### SURFACE

▶ Large clear glass salad bowl

▶ 4 small clear glass salad bowls

## Paint = Liquitex Glossies

Maroon

Blue

Pine Green

Black

Orange

Yellow

Red

Blue + Maroon (3:1)

White

These full-size patterns may be hand-traced or photocopied for personal use only.

# Checkerboard Trim

**1** Clean and prepare your glass bowl as instructed in chapter one.

Cut your Miracle Sponge into a square approximately ½ inch (12mm) in size, and drop it into water. Squeeze the water out as shown on page 19.

Mix Blue and Maroon (3:1), adding more or less Maroon depending on your personal preference. Be sure the little sponge square is wrung out well. Press it on a paper towel if need be, before loading the paint.

Load the full edge of the sponge into the Blue and Maroon mixture; then sideload the sponge into White.

**2** Begin by lining up the top edge of the sponge exactly with the top edge of the bowl. For the second row, line up the top left corner of the sponge with the bottom right corner of the first row. Don't try to make this perfect or you'll just drive yourself crazy. Reload the sponge with paint about every 4 or 5 squares.

# Flowers

**3** Continue around the bowl and you may find that as you near the end of your rows, the checks may not fit exactly. Now is the time when you can adjust the spacing. Bring the squares in a little closer to each other, or space them out just a little, whatever makes the rows complete.

**4** To simplify the placement of your patterns, make four copies of the flower pattern and four copies of the cherry pattern. Trim the paper close to the pattern lines. Decide where you want the first flower and tape this pattern to the inside of the bowl. Then divide the bowl into quarters and tape another flower directly across from the first. Do the same with your other two flowers. Again, this doesn't have to be perfect. You don't have to trace the pattern onto the glass—you will see it through the bowl.

**5** Paint the petals using your no. 8 filbert with White. Start on the outside edge of the petal and pull in toward the flower center, making a kind of heart shape. Press and release quickly and easily, two strokes per petal.

**6** To shade most petals, let the White dry, then make a sideload float of Black on your no. 8 filbert, thinned with water. Don't shade every petal.

**7** Stipple in the centers with a little bit of Yellow on your no. 14 Langnickel. Dry thoroughly with a hair dryer before proceeding.

# Flowers and Cherries

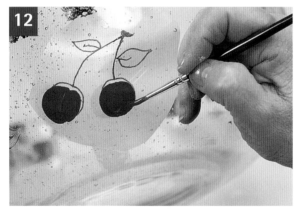

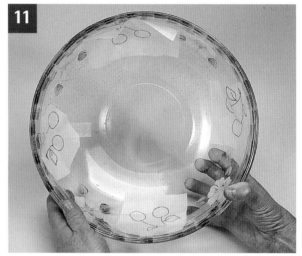

**9** Double load your no. 2 filbert with Pine Green and a touch of White (drag the edge of your brush through the White). Apply a leaf stroke. If the leaves are transparent in some areas, this is fine. It helps them look more highlighted.

**10** Randomly apply Black dots with a dulled toothpick. Have some dots falling on the petals and some on the center, be sure they aren't in a straight line.

**11** Tape the four cherry patterns to the inside of the bowl as you did the flower patterns.

**12** Fill in the cherry shapes using your no. 5 round and Red.

**8** Side load with just a little bit of Orange and stipple along the lower edge of the flower center. If you get a little too much Orange, just go back and fill in with more Yellow. Dab just a bit of White at the upper left edge for a strong highlight.

# Finishing Up

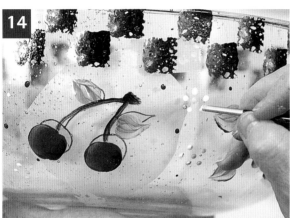

**13** With the same brush, paint in the stems using Brown. Now double load your no. 4 flat with Red, dragging a corner through White. Highlight the left sides of the cherries.

**14** Using the Maroon and Blue mixture with a touch of White, add dots randomly with the handle end of your brush. Use White (and Yellow for the centers) to make five-dot flowers (five White dots in a circle with one Yellow dot in the middle). Keep checking as you dot to make sure the paint doesn't run.

**15** Allow all the paint to dry and bake the bowl in your oven according to the paint manufacturer's instructions.

# *Snowman*
# Plate

Christmas dishes are so popular and it's really fun to be able to create your own unique set. This design is painted on the back of a clear glass plate. With the design showing through the food can be served on the plate.

When painting the reverse glass technique, it's best to paint multiples of the same design as each stage of painting must completely dry before going on to the next step. If you are doing a set of eight plates, you would do each step on all eight. By the time the eighth plate is finished the first plate would be dry and ready for the next step. This saves a lot of time and work and you'll be surprised how an entire place setting of dishes can be completed in one painting session.

## Paint = Liquitex Glossies

Maroon

Red

Orange

Green

Black

Brown

Blue Purple

Metallic Gold

White

Orange + Red
(1:1)

Black + Blue Purple
(1:1)

## Materials

### ROYAL BRUSHES

▶ Series 5005, nos. 10 and 14 Langnickel sable

▶ Series 225, no. 5 sable round

▶ Series 599, no. 0 White Taklon liner

### LEFRANC & BOURGEOIS BRUSHES

▶ Glass & Tile brush, no. 4 flat, natural hair

### ADDITIONAL SUPPLIES

▶ rubbing alcohol

▶ permanent fine-point pen

▶ toothpicks

### SURFACE

▶ 9-inch (23cm) or 10-inch (25cm) clear glass plate

▶ 6-inch (15cm) clear salad plate

The plates can be purchased from any craft, variety or home decor store.

These patterns may be hand-traced or photocopied for personal use only. Enlarge at 143% to bring them up to full size.

# Beginning in Reverse

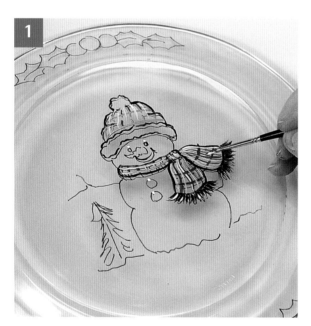

**1** Prepare the glass surface (see page 10) and tape the pattern to the back of the plate. With your permanent pen trace the pattern onto the front of the plate. Turn the plate over and paint on the back. Since you are working in reverse on the back of this plate, there are several items that must be painted in first. Paint in the following order using your no. 0 liner brush:

The highlights in the snowman's eyes and on the buttons using White.

Outline the scarf, hat, body of the snowman, and the mouth with Black. Add a small amount of Black fringe to the scarf. Allow to dry.

Paint the red and white stripes in the scarf by double-loading your no. 0 liner brush using Red with a slice of White. Place individual white stripes between the red stripes.

Stroke in the red fringe on the scarf with Red. You can stroke over the Black if you wish—the black will still show.

Make the green and white stripes on the hat by double-loading the brush with Green plus a slice of White. Next add some White stripes between the Green stripes. Allow all to thoroughly dry before proceeding to the next step.

# Snowman and the Tree

**2** Mix Orange and Red (1:1). Dab your no. 10 Langnickel into this mixture; then dab the tip of the brush into a touch of White and blend it on your palette. Dab the snowman's cheeks on in a dabbing-jabbing motion. Try to avoid the nose as much as possible. With the no. 0 liner and Brown, outline the nose by outlining the bottom and painting in little lines. Highlight the top of the nose with White. Fill in the buttons and the eyes with Black using your no. 0 liner. Paint over the top of your White highlights. Dry thoroughly.

**3** Use your no. 10 Langnickel to paint in the Red hat; exclude the pom-pom and the cuff. With the Red paint still in the brush, side load into Maroon and pounce in some Maroon on the hat next to the cuff. Now wash out your brush. Load the brush with Green and fill in the scarf, covering the stripes. For the cuff on the hat, double load with the Green and White and pounce the color on, keeping the White at the top. Do the same with the pom-pom on the top of the hat.

Fill in the nose with Orange using your no. 8 round. Just dab this in to cover it and then dry thoroughly.

**4** With your no. 14 Langnickel, dab White on the snowman. Don't go all the way to the edge—keep the shaded areas uncovered; you will come back and shade these in the next step.

**5** Mix Blue Purple and Black (1:1) and using the same brush, double load this mixture with White. While the White on the snowman is still wet from the last step, stipple the dark color into the areas you left uncovered. Turn the plate over periodically to see how the shading looks from the front—it should look soft and blended. Pounce in White snow under the snowman and shade with the Blue Purple and Black mix.

**6** To paint the tree, double load Green plus a little White on your no. 10 Langnickel. Start at the top and pounce in the tree shape. Triple load your brush by also adding some of the Blue Purple and Black mixture, then add some shading to the tree.

# Snowflakes and Holly

**7** With your no. 0 liner and Brown, paint in the twig arm. Shade the under side of the arm with Black if you like. Add White snowflakes with your liner by simply painting two longer lines crossed over with two shorter lines as shown.

**8** Finish with dots on the tip of each line using your dulled toothpick. While you have White on the toothpick, dab a little snow on the snowman's arm. Dry thoroughly.

**9** Once the painted area is completely dry, turn the plate over and transfer the pattern to the rim as you did in Project 1 (see page 26). You will now be painting the rim on the front of the plate. Use your no. 8 round and basecoat the berries with Red and the leaves with Green. Add a second coat to the berries. Be sure the first coat is thoroughly dry!

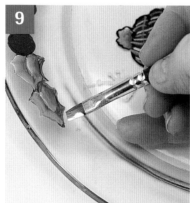
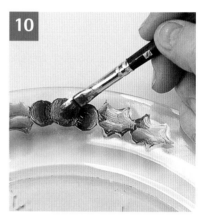

Double load your no. 4 flat with Green tipped into White. Keep the White facing the outside edge of the plate and highlight the leaves. Also highlight the leaf centers as shown.

**10** Float Black shading on the two half berries next to the center berry. Float just a tiny bit on the bottom right side of the center berry.

Double load Red with a touch of White and highlight the berries as shown.

**11** With White on your liner brush, finish the snowflakes on the rim. Float Metallic Gold with your no. 4 flat brush to enhance the holly a bit.

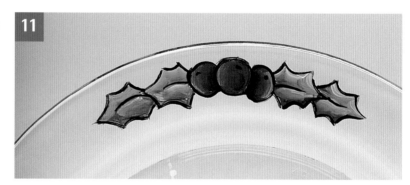

**12** Using your dulled toothpick, dab on flowers of three White dots and one Metallic Gold dot in the center. Also dot on random accent dots where you see fit.

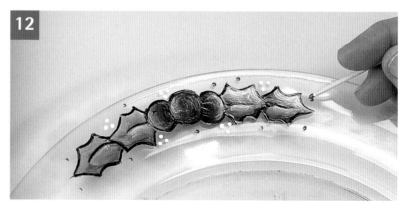

# Finishing

**13** Once the plate is completely dry, bake it in the oven according to the paint manufacturer's instructions. Remember, when baking glass painted with the reverse technique, turn the plate over so the painted area is facing up, allowing heat to circulate.

# Salad Plate and Mug

## Salad Plate Instructions:

**1** Place a Green lifeline all around the outer and inner rim of the front side of the plate. Remember it's okay to break the line and make two dots when you think you are running out of paint.
**2** Place White snowflakes randomly around the rim of the plate.
**3** Make dots of Red around the green lifeline.
**4** Place a dot on each curve of the line.

## Instructions for other pieces:

When painting a mug or other clear glass pieces that are painted on the front, use the same techniques as for the Snowman plate and paint in the following order:
**1** Snowman head and body: Paint and shade using same brush and same technique as on the plate. Let dry.
**2** Basecoat the hat Red. Shade next to the scarf.
**3** Basecoat the scarf Green. Pounce fur on the hat and pom-pom. Let dry.
**4** Complete the cheeks, nose, eyes and mouth as you did on the plate. Fill in the buttons with Black.
**5** Apply stripes on the scarf and hat using the same colors as on the plate. Stroke fringe on the scarf.
**6** Paint the twig arm and the tree the same as on the plate.
**7** Outline the entire design in Black.
**8** Apply White snowflakes and snow on the ground. Let dry.
**9** Paint decorative holly trim as you did on the plate.

# *Strawberry*
# Bowl

Strawberries are very easy to paint, and they are so fresh and pretty on white china bowls. I found these bowls at a department store in the mall, but similar ones are available in almost all the craft and discount stores that I have visited. The design can be adjusted to fit any size bowl.

## Paint = Liquitex Glossies

Yellow

Red

Pine Green

Maroon

Blue Purple

Blue

White

Blue + Blue Purple
(1:1)

## Materials

### ROYAL BRUSHES

▷ Series 599, no. 0 White Taklon liner
  or Series 225, no. 0 sable round

▷ Series 599, no. 5/0 and no. 2
  White Taklon liner

▷ Series 150, no. 8 White Taklon shader

▷ Series 179, nos. 2, 4 and 6 White Taklon
  cats tongue (filbert)

▷ Series 5005, nos. 10, 12 and 14
  Langnickel sable

### ADDITIONAL SUPPLIES

▷ wax-free transfer paper

▷ ballpoint pen or stylus

▷ rubbing alcohol

▷ toothpicks

▷ lint-free paper towels

### SURFACE

▷ White china bowl from craft, hobby, or
  home goods store.

This pattern may be hand-traced or photocopied for personal use only. Enlarge at 143% to bring it up to full size.

# Basecoat the Strawberries

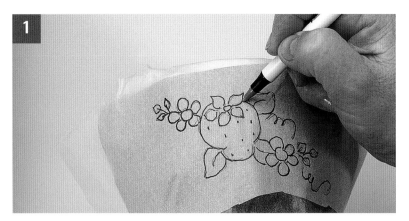

**1** Wash, rinse and dry the white china bowl; then wipe with rubbing alcohol and a lint-free paper towel. Transfer the pattern onto the bowl and with wax-free transfer paper place the strawberry designs equally around the bowl. Add as many or as few as you like.

**2** Basecoat the entire strawberry using your no. 8 shader and Red paint. Cover the entire fruit area. Don't try to paint around the bract pattern. The bracts will be painted on top once the strawberry base-coat dries. Dry thoroughly.

# Shading and Highlighting

**3** Double load your shader with Red and Maroon and shade the upper left side of the strawberry. Begin at the top and slide down around the fat part of the strawberry; then slide into the berry with the chisel edge of your brush. Shade the bottom part, using short brushstrokes just inside of the edge. Let dry.

**4** Double load your no. 12 or no. 14 Langnickel brush with Yellow and Red. Pounce in a circle, keeping the Yellow toward the middle of the berry and Red toward the outside edges. Pouncing in a somewhat ragged fashion makes the strawberries look more realistic. Dry thoroughly.

Sometimes the Yellow does not show up well enough and needs to be reapplied. The yellow area will have to be wide enough to accommodate a final highlight of White, so use it generously. (See the highlighting instructions on page 15 for an optional but very effective method of drybrushing in a highlight.)

**5** Using your no. 12 or no. 14 Langnickel, dip into White, then tap on a paper towel to remove any excess paint. Drybrush using a light tapping motion to apply White into the center of the Yellow highlight.

When placing highlights, here's a little rhyme to help you: "If it looks too light, it's just right. If it looks just right, it's not right."

**6** Load your no. 2 filbert with Pine Green and side load with White. Apply each bract with one stroke, press and pull to a point. The brush will make the shape easily for you. The center of the top is painted with just a touch.

## Hint

For left-handers, it may be easier for you to shade the right side of the strawberry. Keep the shaded sides consistent—either all on the right or all on the left.

# Seeds and Flowers

**7** With Yellow and your dulled toothpick, apply the seeds with a short touch-and-pull motion.

**8** To accent the seeds, paint a thin Black line on the left side of each seed. The Black line needs to be much thinner than the Yellow. This creates a slight shadow next to each seed. Place a tiny white dot in the upper right corner of the yellow seed as a final highlight.

**9** Load your no. 4 filbert brush half with Blue and half with Blue Purple. Create each flower petal with one stroke by pressing and lifting from the outside edge of the petal to the center. Use the flat edge of the filbert brush and pull in. Do not wash the brush.

   Using the same brush, dip into White. Add White to each petal using the chisel edge of your brush, two strokes per petal. Leave a tiny bit of the blue showing around the center.

**10** Using your no. 10 Langnickel, tap a tiny bit of Yellow into the flower center. Then tap in just a bit of Maroon toward the bottom before the Yellow dries. Touch in just a dab of White highlighting at the top of the center.

# Leaves

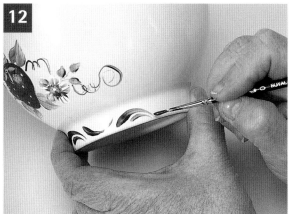

**11** Double load your no. 6 filbert with Green and White and stroke in the leaf using the two-stroke leaf technique (see page 17). Use your no. 2 filbert to do the smaller leaves using the same technique. Sometimes add a little more Green, sometimes a little more White to your mixture so your leaves don't all look the same.

**12** Using Green thinned with water or thinner and your 5/0 liner brush, follow the pattern lines for the curlicues—or freehand in your own using the "*e*'s and *m*'s" technique shown on page 16. Curlicues are much prettier and easier when free-handed, as it is difficult to follow an exact pattern with a liner brush on china. Make the comma strokes on the bottom of the bowl with your no. 2 liner—just press and pull. Alternate two cradled comma strokes pointing down, then one comma stroke pointing up. Repeat this pattern as you circle the bowl.

**13** Let the paint dry completely, then bake the finished bowl according to the paint manufacturer's instructions.

# *Dressing*
# Table Set

These pieces of glass were all purchased at a crafts store except for the perfume bottle, which I bought at a dollar shop. I had so much fun painting this design that I just could not stop. This pretty and feminine dressing table set would make a wonderful gift for a young lady or a new bride. I hope you enjoy painting it as much as I did.

## Paint = Liquitex Glossies

| | | | |
|---|---|---|---|
| Red Purple | Maroon | Pine Green | Purple |

| | | |
|---|---|---|
| Yellow | White | Red Purple + White (3:1) |

## Materials

### ROYAL BRUSHES

▷ Series 5005, no. 10 or 12 Langnickel sable

▷ Series 159, nos. 2 and 8 White Taklon flat

▷ Series 179, nos. 2 and 8 White Taklon cats tongue (filbert)

▷ Series 599, no. 5/0 and no. 2 White Taklon liner

### ADDITIONAL SUPPLIES

▷ wax-free transfer paper

▷ ballpoint pen or stylus

▷ rubbing alcohol

▷ Scotch Magic Tape

▷ toothpicks

▷ lint-free paper towels

### SURFACE

▷ Glass jar and/or miscellaneous dressing table items from any craft, hobby or variety store.

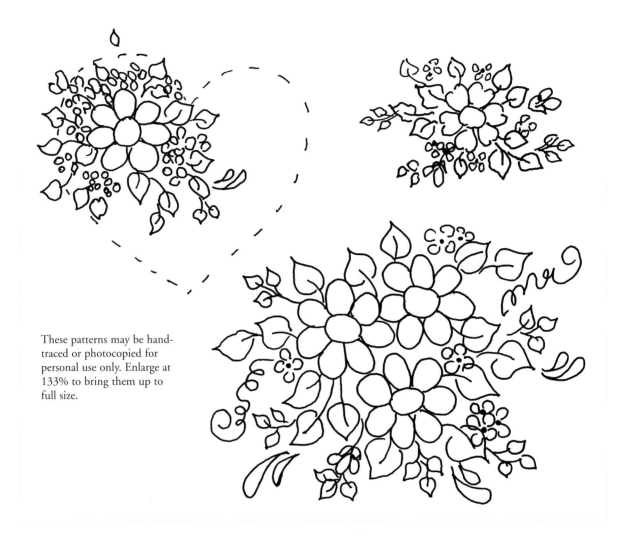

These patterns may be hand-traced or photocopied for personal use only. Enlarge at 133% to bring them up to full size.

# Flower Petals

**1** Wash, rinse and dry the glass piece; then wipe with rubbing alcohol and a lint-free paper towel. Transfer the pattern onto the glass.

Using Red Purple and White (3:1) and your no. 8 filbert, paint in each flower petal with one stroke from the outside edge to the center. Don't worry if you get a little of this color on the center—it will be covered up with Yellow. Dry thoroughly.

# Flower Petals continued

## Hint

When washing out your brush, make sure you use clean water and blot your brush really well on a paper towel. You may find that the brush has a tinge of your last color in it, but that's okay; the White Taklon hairs are sometimes stained by the more intense paint colors.

**2** Using your no. 8 flat brush, double load with Maroon and the pink mixture from step 1. Place the Maroon side of the brush next to the center and shade the inside of each petal. To lay the shading on, tap and press the brush. The double-loaded brush will give a soft shading and a nice variation of color.

**3** Still using the same brush, tip it into White. Start at the outside edge of each petal and pull lightly into the middle. Make sure to use a very light touch; you want variations in the lightness and darkness of each petal. If you reload your brush for every other petal, this variation will happen easily.

**4** Using your no. 8 flat, basecoat in Purple using the same stroke method as you did in step 1. Dry thoroughly. You won't need to dab the darker center in as you did on the pink flowers since you are starting with a darker base color already.

Now dip the same brush into White and starting at the outside edge, pull into the middle for highlighting as you did on the pink flowers.

**5** Highlight the petals on the outer edges with White using your no. 8 flat brush wherever you like. This makes the petals appear to have more zip.

# Flowers and Leaves

**6** With your no. 10 or 12 Langnickel, load Yellow (remember to always add a touch of White to the Yellow to make it more opaque) and dab in the flower centers. Pick up a touch of Maroon and dab this in toward the center bottom to create slight shading. Wash out your brush and apply a White highlight. (See step 5 on page 45 for the highlighting technique.) Dry thoroughly.

**7** Double load your no. 8 flat with Pine Green and White. Create each leaf using the two-stroke leaf method (see page 17). Keep the White on the top of the brush each time.

**8** Double load your no. 2 flat with Purple, tipping the edge of the brush into White. Add some filler flowers by just laying the brush on the glass and pivoting, creating half circles. Make each little petal this way (see page 18). Make some of the flowers using the pink mixture (see step 1) tipped in White. It's good to have these flowers vary in color—some more white, some more purple or pink.

**9** To paint the tiny filler leaves, use your no. 2 filbert with Pine Green and White. These leaves are made with one stroke on the chisel edge of your brush—just push and pull. Keep White on the top of the brush (see page 17).

# Leaf Stems and Curlicues

**10** Mix Pine Green with a touch of Purple (thinned with water) to darken. With your no. 5/0 liner, paint the curlicues in a loose and carefree manner following the pattern. Also paint the stems on the leaves and the comma strokes using this same paint mixture. Each filler flower has four little yellow dots in the center—use a dulled toothpick to fill these in. Dot in little White dots as shown.

**11** The top of the jar is painted with alternating dip-dot flowers of Purple, then Pink. Look at the top of the jar as if it were a clockface and place a Pink flower at 12 o'clock, one at 6, one at 3 and one at 9. Then place a Purple flower evenly spaced between each Pink flower. Add three leaves on the sides of each flower using your no. 2 filbert. Embellish with white dots.

**12** Paint the rim of the mirror with alternating dip-dot flowers using a slightly dulled toothpick to make them very small. Make the leaves on each side of the flowers with dots placed on with a dulled toothpick. Dot on the paint; then slide it outward to a point to form a leaf.

The perfume bottles and the heart box are painted the same as the canister. Use the smaller patterns and adjust them to fit.

Allow all the pieces to dry, then bake them according to the paint manufacturer's instructions.

# *Blue Glass*
# Vase

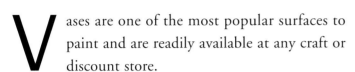

Vases are one of the most popular surfaces to paint and are readily available at any craft or discount store.

I chose blue glass, but this design would also be beautiful on a clear glass vase.

Once you learn how to paint this simple and fun floral design, you won't need to follow a pattern. But for those who are a little unsure, I have included the pattern for you.

## Paint = Liquitex Glossies

Green

Yellow Orange

Yellow

White

Blue

## Materials

**ROYAL BRUSHES**

▶ Series 159, no. 6 White Taklon flat

▶ Series 599, no. 0 White Taklon liner

▶ Series 179, no. 2
White Taklon cats tongue (filbert)

**ADDITIONAL SUPPLIES**

▶ white or yellow wax-free transfer paper

▶ ballpoint pen or stylus

▶ toothpicks

▶ Q-tips

▶ rubbing alcohol

▶ lint-free paper towels

**SURFACE**

▶ Blue glass vase from any craft, hobby or home decor store.

This pattern may be hand-traced or photocopied for personal use only. Enlarge at 118% to bring it up to full size.

# Petals

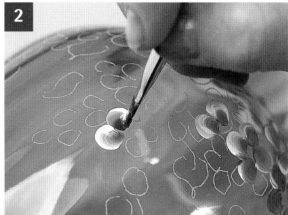

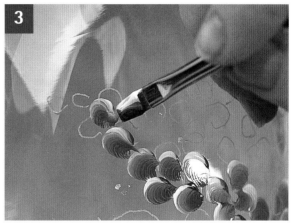

**1** Wash, rinse and dry the vase; then wipe with rubbing alcohol on a lint-free paper towel. When transferring this pattern onto the vase, it helps if you cut (notch) the pattern at the top and bottom before you tape it on so the paper will conform better to the roundness of the vase. Trace the pattern on using white or yellow wax-free transfer paper. Turn the pattern in whichever direction it best fits your vase. You can have as many or as few flowers on your project as you want.

**2** With your no. 6 flat, double load Blue and White. Place the brush on the chisel edge and press and pivot the brush in a half circle. Be sure to keep the White facing the outer edge of the petal at all times.

You can pivot the brush in a clockwise or counter-clockwise direction, whichever is more comfortable for you. Keep the brush on the surface throughout the stroke. Don't let up on the bristles too quickly, you want a round petal (not a half circle shape).

**3** Notice that the trailing flowers are made in exactly the same manner as the full flower in step 2. Fill these in one petal at a time. You can go in after the Blue dries and add more White on any flower that you think might need more.

Sometimes these flowers have one petal, sometimes two petals. You don't have to overlap them; they all have their own space. Just keep this simple and enjoy the process.

## Hint

These flowers are quick and easy, and once you learn how to paint them, you may not ever want to paint another type of flower. You'll be a four-petal flower pro by the time you finish this project.

# Leaves and Filler Flowers

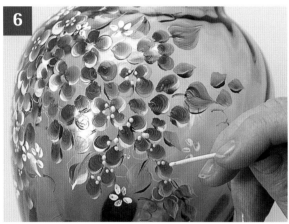

**4** With your no. 6 flat, double load White and Green and paint the leaves using the two-stroke leaf method described on page 17. Be sure to pull some leaves up onto the neck of the vase.

**5** Using your no. 2 filbert, add White filler flowers at the base of each leaf and randomly around the blue flowers. These are five-petal flowers formed by gently touching the chisel edge of your brush to the glass and then lifting. Sometimes you may not have room for all five petals—that's okay, they can just be half flowers if you want.

**6** Add curlicues with Green and a touch of White (be sure to thin the paint) on your no. 0 liner—lots of curlicues make the vase look extra special. You'll need to thin your paint with water or thinning medium. Add stems on some of the leaves. The centers of the blue flowers are Yellow with a touch of White dotted on with a dulled toothpick. Dot four or five dots on the full flower centers and fewer dots on the trailing flowers.

**7** Add one dot into the center of the white flowers with Yellow Orange paint. Once the paint is completely dry, remove the pattern lines with a dry Q-tip or a dry soft tissue. Do not use water or alcohol to remove the pattern.

**8**

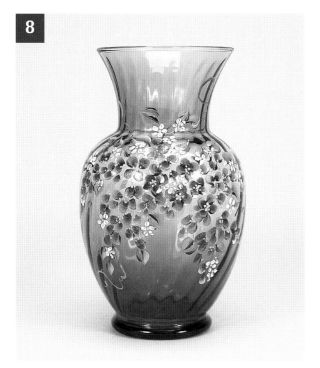

**8** After all the paint has dried completely, bake your vase in the oven according to the paint manufacturer's instructions.

# *Wedding*

# Roses

T his would make a lovely gift for a soon-to-be bride. At least two place settings plus the glass vase could be included in a gift of celebration. I can assure you, however, that the bride will never give up her request for more place settings, so be prepared to give the gift that keeps on giving.

## Paint = Liquitex Glossies

Red Purple

Maroon

Green

Silver

Blue

White

Red Purple + White
(1:1) (Medium Pink)

Maroon + Red Purple
(1:1)

Green + Light Pink
Mixture (3:1)

Green + Maroon
(4:1)

## Materials

### ROYAL BRUSHES

▷ Series 225, no. 8 sable round

▷ Series 159-S, no. 2
white Taklon blender (bright)

▷ Series 599, no. 0 white Taklon liner

▷ Series 179, no. 2
White Taklon cats tongue (filbert)

### ADDITIONAL SUPPLIES

▷ wax-free transfer paper

▷ ballpoint pen or stylus

▷ toothpicks

### SURFACE

▷ Clear plates and/or glassware
from any craft supply, hobby
or home goods store.

These patterns may be hand-traced or photocopied for personal use only. Enlarge the top pattern (for the charger) and the bottom pattern (for the plate) at 143% to bring them up to full size.

# Ribbon and Roses

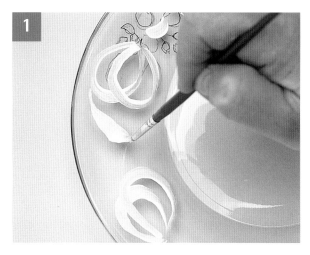

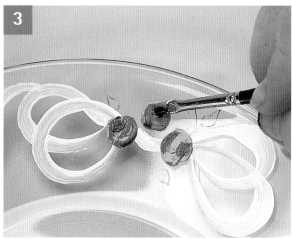

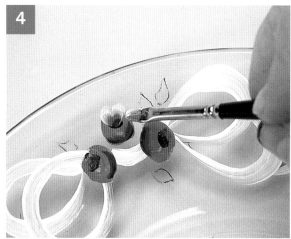

**1** Prepare your surface as previously instructed and trace the pattern onto the top of the plate rim. Use your no. 5 round and a ribbon stroke to paint the ribbon White.

For this stroke start on the brush tip. Press down as you near the middle of the ribbon section, and lift to come to a point (see page 16). One coat is all you need; the transparency is very nice. The glass showing through the paint adds the shading.

Paint all of the ribbon before painting any other areas. If you are doing multiple pieces, paint all the ribbon on each piece before proceeding to the next step. Dry thoroughly.

**2** Mix Red Purple and White (1:1) to make a medium value of pink. With this mixture and the same brush, basecoat the roses in a round ball shape as shown. Only one coat is needed, as you will be painting over this area. Dry thoroughly.

**3** Using your no. 2 bright and a mixture of Red Purple and Maroon (1:1), float in the bowl and bottom of the rose. Be aware of the positioning of the roses as you float in the bowl: The top rose points up and the side roses point outward to the sides. Your rose will not look perfect at this point.

**4** Now comes the fun part. Remember the blossom strokes we used for the little filler flowers in the blue vase project (page 58). You will be using the same strokes for the area above the bowl of the rose. Double load your no. 2 bright with White on one side and the medium pink mixture on the other. Blend the brush on the palette to make sure the colors blend together with a good, strong white edge. Paint just two of the blossom strokes above the bowl of the rose.

# Roses, Leaves and Dip Dots

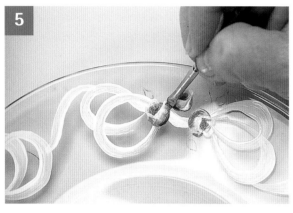

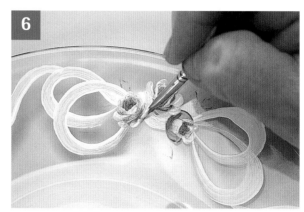

**5** With the White on the upper edge of the double-loaded brush, slide down the left side of the bowl shape. Push down straight across the bottom of the bowl shape and chisel up the right side. The White should rest right next to the dark center. This will form the front petal of the rose.

**6** Next, with the same double-loaded brush, apply five little chisel-pull strokes to finish this little rose. (See page 18 for more detailed instructions for this stroke.)

**7** For the little green leaves, use your no. 2 filbert and Green mixed with the pink mix from step 2. Touch the side of your brush into White, then use a pull stroke to form the leaves, one stroke per leaf.

**8** Mix Green with just enough Maroon to make a color darker than your other leaves. With your no. 0 liner, touch on and lift to form tiny filler leaves.

**9** With a dulled toothpick, dot White around the leaves and Silver around the ribbon. If you find you like the ribbon without the Silver dots, feel free to leave them off. Make this your project.

# Other Pieces

**10** Bake your Wedding Roses plate according to the paint manufacturer's instructions.

**11** To paint the wine glass and the vase, follow the directions for the plate and adjust the pattern to fit.

For the white china charger, use the same colors and techniques as on the glass plate. It is easier to mark this pattern with a marking pencil than to try to trace a pattern on. Placement of the roses is the most important step, as all the leaves and strokes are placed around the rose itself. Follow these easy directions for marking the pattern and refer to the drawing example on page 62.

Draw a small circle on the top rim of the plate for the first rose. Move over 1 inch (2.5cm) and draw another circle. Then draw a circle for a rose on the bottom rim of the plate. Alternate drawing circles on the top rim and bottom rim, keeping the spacing about 1 inch (2.5cm) apart.

Place strokes around the roses with Green. Follow the pattern to see the flow of the design, making two strokes on each side of each rose. Make the leaves using your no. 2 filbert. I added some blue filler flowers made with a rounded toothpick and a mixture of equal parts Blue and White. Dot Yellow for the center. Dot White randomly around the leaves for filler.

# *Fruit*
# Tiles

Have you always wanted to have hand-painted tiles in your home? Well, now you can paint your own. They're easier than you think, and they're just the thing to brighten up your kitchen. You could also make them as a special housewarming gift.

You can frame these tiles to make a large trivet or decorative tray or use them individually as coasters.

## Materials

### ROYAL BRUSHES

▶ Series 599, no. 5/0 White Taklon liner

▶ Series 159, nos. 6 and 8  White Taklon flat

▶ Series 179, nos. 4 and 8 White Taklon cats tongue (filbert)

▶ Series 5005 nos. 8 and 14 or 16 Langnickel sable

### ADDITIONAL SUPPLIES

▶ wax-free transfer paper

▶ ballpoint pen or stylus

▶ rubbing alcohol

▶ old toothbrush

▶ sheet of paper

### SURFACE

▶ 4-inch (10cm) square white tiles from any craft supply or tile store.

## Paint = Liquitex Glossies

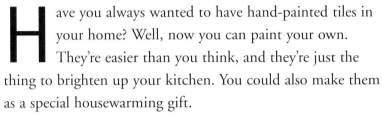

| | | | |
|---|---|---|---|
| Yellow | Maroon | Green | Brown |

| | | | |
|---|---|---|---|
| Black | Purple | Blue | Orange |

| | | | |
|---|---|---|---|
| White | Pine Green | Maroon + touch of Yellow | Yellow + touch of Green |

| | | | |
|---|---|---|---|
| Orange + touch of White | Purple + White (1:1) | Blue + Purple (1:1) + touch of White | Last mix + more White |

Pine Green + Purple (1:1)

These patterns may be hand-traced or photo-copied for personal use only. Enlarge at 118% to bring them up to full size.

# Pear Tile

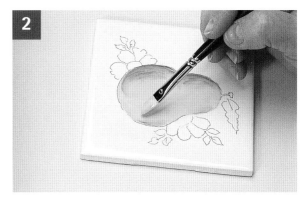

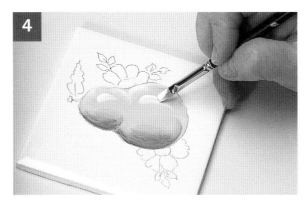

**1** Clean the surface with rubbing alcohol and a lint-free paper towel. Trace on the pattern using wax-free transfer paper and a ballpoint pen or stylus.

Mix Yellow (with a tiny touch of White) and using your no. 8 filbert, basecoat, making shape-following strokes. Try to stay inside the pattern lines so you can remove these afterward. (If the pattern smudges, stop and clean it up with a Q-tip barely moistened with rubbing alcohol.) Dry thoroughly before proceeding.

For the shading or "blush" on the pear, mix Maroon with a touch of Yellow to make a blush mix. Double load your no. 8 filbert with Yellow and the blush mix. This is treated similarly to the shading on the strawberry (see page 15). Beginning at the top on the left side of the pear (lefties on the right), slide your brush down and curve in slightly (see photo). Make a second curve on the bottom half, not quite going all the way to the bottom of the pear. Walk your brush in to bring the blush in a bit more from the edge. Be careful not to work this too much. On the right side of the pear, make another small curve close to the bottom as shown. Keep this very light.

**2** Notice the hint of Green on the right side about ¼-inch (0.6cm) in from the outside edge of the pear. Mix a tiny bit of Green with Yellow, and double load your no. 8 filbert with Yellow and the mixture, keeping the Green facing toward the pear edge. Make this a very light application as it is just a tint. Place the tint next to the blush that was previously applied; the tint will be much lighter. Let dry.

**3** Using the same brush, float White on the outside edge of the right side of the pear. Float around the top half and curve in. Then float around the bottom half, fading away as you reach the bottom. Be careful not to get this too light; you still have to paint the highlight. Dry thoroughly.

**4** Before you highlight make sure you are happy with the blending of your blush mix and Yellow and adjust as needed. For the highlight, side load the no. 6 flat brush with White and a small amount of water. Blend the paint three-quarters of the way across the brush, not just halfway. You want this to be a strong highlight.

Float the highlight on the right side of the pear in the rounded area. Refer to the photo above.

# Pear Tile continued

**5** Still using your no. 6 flat side loaded with Brown, float a shadow following the pattern for the blossom end shadow. Hold the brush with the brown edge pointed in and the clean edge pointed toward the edge of the pear. Dry thoroughly.

**6** Using your no. 5/0 liner brush and thinned Black, paint in the little hairs inside the shadow. Be sure not to add too many. If the hairs on the blossom end are too heavy or harsh, you can add a little White over the top of them to soften.

**7** Using Brown, paint in the stem with your liner. Quickly paint in Black underneath the cut-end and a little White right above it.

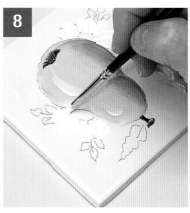

**8** Load your no. 4 filbert with White, but don't fill it too full. Create each daisy petal using two strokes on the chisel edge of your brush (see page 18).

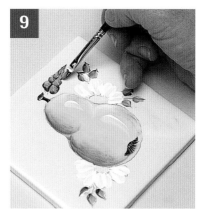

**9** While the petals are drying, fill in the daisy leaves using the same brush double loaded with Green and White. Paint one-stroke leaves. Reload for each leaf. Let the White fall wherever it lands. Next paint in the pear leaf, but for this keep the White facing up.

**10** With your no. 8 sable, tap in the daisy centers with Yellow. While still wet, add Maroon to one side of the brush. Tap this darker side next to the pear.

**11** After the daisies are completely dried, give them personality by lightly outlining them using your no. 5/0 liner with Black thinned with water. (This helps distinguish them from the white of the tile.) Pull a stem from the pear stem to the leaf using the thinned black. Finally, add the dots. You will be painting the daisies on all four tiles using these same steps.

**12** To flyspeck the pear, load an old toothbrush with thinned Brown. Run your finger over top of the toothbrush and first fly speck a piece of paper to see what direction the paint is spattering. Then hold the brush above the pear and spatter it. You can either cut a hole in a piece of paper to protect the white tile area, or carefully wipe the tile off afterward with a little water.

# Apple Tile

**13** Using Red and your no. 8 flat, basecoat your apple with shape-following strokes (refer to page 14). Dry thoroughly.

Float Brown with your no. 6 flat brush into the indention in the stem end. This is done in the same way as the shading on the bottom of the pear.

Add Orange and a tiny bit of White to your no. 14 or 16 sable brush. Flatten out the bristles as shown.

**14** Lightly streak down the apple, barely skimming the surface. Try to use a touch so light it's like you're not even touching it. Do this in front of and behind the shading (on the top). Keep your touch as light as possible. When you think you have enough, apply a little more. Thin the mix if needed.

**15** Using Yellow and White (1:1), streak in the bright, final highlight using the same technique as you used in step 14. Use a light, light, light touch.

# Apple Tile continued

**16** Side load your no. 8 flat with Maroon, blending the paint three-quarters of the way across the brush. Float Maroon around the sides of the apple. Darken the shadow a bit at the stem end of the apple. Let this coat dry thoroughly.

**17** Reinforce the shading by following the instructions in step 14, floating Maroon again. This may look a little dark right now, but once all the other colors are around it, you'll find it looks just right. Finish the flowers and leaves as you did for the pear.

# Grapes Tile

**18** Using your no. 6 flat, base in Purple on the grapes using shape-following strokes. Leave openings between the grapes and dry thoroughly. Apply a second coat of the Purple, still allowing the space between the grapes. Dry thoroughly.

**19** Mix Purple and White (1:1). Double load your no. 6 flat with Purple and the Purple and White mixture. You can see by the photo where I placed the highlights, but you can use your own discretion and place more or less wherever you like. Dry thoroughly.

**20** Mix Blue and Purple (1:1) with a touch of White. With the same brush, float this bluish mixture on the grapes as shown. Dry thoroughly.

**21** Add more White to the last mix. Float this mixture to create just a little more lightness and highlighting. Dry thoroughly.

**22** Now use your no. 5/0 liner brush to touch a small white stroke to most of the grapes. Use your own creativity to make these grapes appear the way you like them.

**23** Mix Purple and Pine Green (1:3). With your no. 8 flat, basecoat the leaves using a shape-following stroke. You will need two coats, so allow the first coat to dry thoroughly before proceeding with the second coat.

**24** Double load your no. 8 flat with the Purple and Green mixture and White. Drag this around the leaves to highlight the edges. Outline the leaves with Black using your no. 5/0 liner brush. This will clean up the edges. Add daisies.

# Finishing

**25** Paint the strawberry tile exactly as you did the strawberry on the bowl (see pages 44-47). Finish the daisies and leaves as you did for the other three tiles.

**26** Bake the tiles as instructed by the paint manufacturer. Use the tiles separately or place them in a frame like I've done here. Arrange the tiles any way that you like.

**27** My husband David made this frame for this project. Here are simplified instructions:

The backing is 14 x 14-inch (35cm) ¼-inch (6mm) plywood.

Frame with ¾-inch (19mm) strips cut from ½-inch (12mm) pine. Use a router with a ¼-inch (6mm) roundover bit to round off the inside and outside edges of the frame.

Glue the back to the routered frame.

# *Kids'*
# Project

T his project is perfect for kids of all ages. We have used a recycled jar to sponge on the butterflies. The jar could be used as a candleholder because its opening is large enough to hold a small glass votive for a candle. Do not place the candle directly in the jar, as the glass could break.

This also makes a great project for scouts, church, play groups and more. Attach a piece of flexible screening or nylon net to the top with a rubber band or ribbon, and the kids could use it for a bug observatory.

Have fun, and let the kids be creative!

## Materials

**SUPPLIES**

▷ Miracle Sponge

▷ scissors

▷ toothpicks

▷ brush handle for dots

▷ wax-free transfer paper

▷ ballpoint pen or stylus

**SURFACE**

▷ Any kind of glass jar.

## Paint = Liquitex Glossies

Green

Yellow

Orange

Blue Purple

White

Pink

Blue

Pine Green

These full-size patterns may be hand-traced or photo-copied for personal use only.

**1** Trace the pattern shapes onto your Miracle Sponge and cut the shapes out. Drop the shapes into the water as described on page 19. It is important that you remove all moisture from your sponges, so I suggest squeezing them between paper towels until every trace of moisture is removed.

# Butterfly

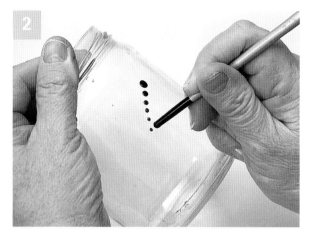

**2** Using fresh paint, dip a brush handle into Blue Purple and make six graduated dots in a slight curve from large to smaller, creating the butterfly body. This gives you a good place to begin your butterfly.

**3** Dip the entire heart-shaped sponge in Blue Purple and dip the rounded tips in White. Dab on your palette to blend.

**4** Press and rock the sponge with your finger.

**5** Dip the oval-shaped sponge (back wing shape) into Blue Purple; place it next to the heart and press. It's fine if you get too much paint on your wing; the wing will just look bigger.

# Butterfly and Tulip

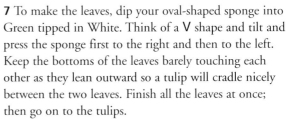

**6** Dip a pointed toothpick into Blue Purple and draw on the antennae. Place a Blue Purple dot on the end of each antenna.

**7** To make the leaves, dip your oval-shaped sponge into Green tipped in White. Think of a V shape and tilt and press the sponge first to the right and then to the left. Keep the bottoms of the leaves barely touching each other as they lean outward so a tulip will cradle nicely between the two leaves. Finish all the leaves at once; then go on to the tulips.

Dip your tulip-shaped sponge in Yellow tipped in White, and apply in the same way to create the blossom. This doesn't have to be perfect (see photo with step 10).

**8** To make the orange butterfly, draw on six more graduated dots with Orange. Again using your heart-shaped sponge, dip the sponge in Orange and dip the rounded part in White. Dab on the palette to blend. Sponge on the orange butterfly as you did the blue one. Add the antennae with Blue Purple. Dry thoroughly.

Once the butterflies are completely dry, use your brush handle again to apply dip-dots to the wings. Add Yellow dots to the orange butterfly and White dots to the blue butterfly.

**9** To create the grass at the bottom, use an extra piece of sponge, pick up Green paint, and tap onto the glass. You can also pick up a little White and tap it over the Green.

**10** Scatter White dots around the flowers. Have an adult bake the jars as instructed by the paint manufacturer.

## Instructions for Flower Jar

Cut circles for the flowers from the Miracle Sponge. It is easier if you cut two circles—one for yellow and one for Blue. Also cut a leaf shape from the Miracle Sponge.

**1** Start with the center of the flower to make placement easier. Dip the circle sponge into Yellow and tip the edge into Pink. Place the sponge in the middle of the jar, leaving enough room to make petals all around.

**2** Dip the circle sponge into Blue, then tip the edge into White. Tap on your palette to distribute the paint, then press onto the jar, making five petals that form a circle around the center. Keep the White edge to the outside. Reload after each petal. Make the leaves with Pine Green dipped into White, and place around the flowers.

**3** Add White dot flowers using the handle of a brush. Dot Yellow into the center. Cut a square in a size that will fit well on your jar and paint the rim with checks as described in the Glass Salad Bowl project (page 30-35).

# *Butterfly*
# Picture Frame

I purchased this china frame and a lamp base at a local arts and crafts supply store. I was surprised to find so many lamps and frames that were perfect for painting, and I was thrilled when I saw how inexpensive they were. This frame would make a perfect gift if you can bear to part with it after it is finished.

## Materials

### ROYAL BRUSHES

▶ Series 179, nos. 2 and 6 White Taklon cats tongue (filbert)

▶ Series 5005, no. 8 Langnickel sable

▶ Series 159, no. 4 White Taklon flat

▶ Series 599, no. 0 White Taklon liner

▶ Series 159-S, no. 4 blender (bright)

### ADDITIONAL SUPPLIES

▶ lint-free paper towels

▶ wax-free transfer paper

▶ ballpoint pen or stylus

▶ toothpicks

### SURFACE

▶ China frame and lamp base from any arts and crafts supply store.

## Paint = Liquitex Glossies

Yellow

Magenta

Blue

Pine Green

Purple

Black

White

White + Magenta
(9:1)

Pine Green + Purple
(9:1)

Magenta + Yellow
(1:1)

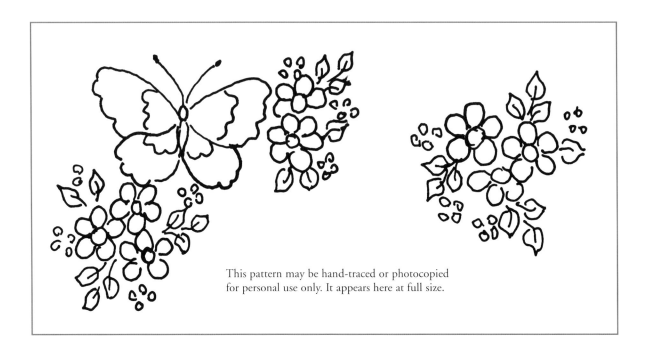

This pattern may be hand-traced or photocopied for personal use only. It appears here at full size.

# Butterfly

**1** Clean the surface with rubbing alcohol and a lint-free paper towel. Trace on the pattern. The pattern on the lamp uses the butterfly motif only in the front with several groupings scattered randomly around. Let the pattern vary. Refer to the photo on page 85 for placement.

Start with White and Magenta (9:1) mixed to a very light pink. With your no. 6 filbert, basecoat the butterfly leaving each section visible as shown. You'll need only one coat. Dry thoroughly.

**2** Using Magenta and your no. 8 Langnickel, begin at the edges of the wings and drag in to the middle. This will look a little messy at this point, but that's okay.

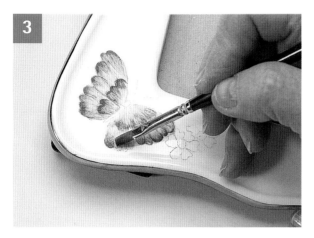

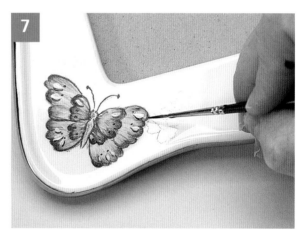

**3** Using your no. 4 flat and Purple, float the edges of the wings using little curved or blossom strokes. Be careful not to get too much Purple on your brush or it will be too dark. Do each section this way.

**4** Still using Purple and the same brush, lightly touch and wiggle a tiny bit of color next to the body.

**5** Use your no. 0 liner brush and Purple to very lightly outline around the edges of the wings and wing sections. Also paint in the little antennae at this time (see photo, step 6).

**6** Still using your liner brush and a mix of Yellow and White (3:1), fill in the body and paint a teardrop shape on the wings. Paint the tiny teardrop with just a touch and pull.

**7** Outline the bottom side of each teardrop with Black. Also fill in the extra dots beside each teardrop.

Mix Magenta and Yellow (1:1) and touch a tiny bit onto the body of the butterfly to highlight. Then, outline the body and the wings lightly with Black.

# Flowers

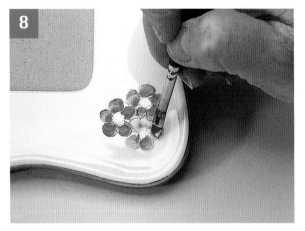

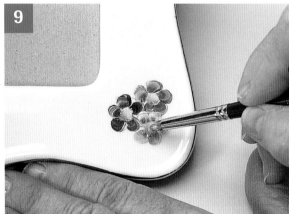

**8** Double load your no. 4 blender first in Blue, then tip the edge in White. Get a really nice edge of White on your brush. Paint some of the flowers on each corner of the frame with Blue using the blossom stroke. Do the same with Purple and White to create some purple flowers. Use Magenta and White to paint the little pink flowers the same way.

**9** With your no. 8 Langnickel, dab in the flower centers first with Yellow. Then mix Magenta and Yellow (1:1) to make a lovely orange color and lightly pounce in the bottoms of the center.

**10** Mix Pine Green and Purple (9:1). Load your no. 2 filbert with this mixture and side load with White to paint one-stroke leaves.

**11** With a pull-touch stroke, paint the smaller leaves with the green mixture on the liner brush (no White added). Paint in the stems with this same mixture. Add tiny Black dots with a pointed toothpick. Paint the White baby's breath dots on the leaves with a dulled toothpick.

## Hint

Enjoy the variations of color. Every petal doesn't have to be the same.

**12** The frame is now complete; there's no need to bake it. It is not necessary to bake these pieces, as they will only be hand washed infrequently and will not get a lot of wear and tear.

**13** You can also use these same instructions to paint a lamp base.

After placing the main butterfly pattern on the lamp, scatter clusters of flowers around the base. Use single flowers to fill in the gaps.

PROJECT 11

# *Ribbons*

# and Roses

R everse glass painting is not difficult—it just makes you think ahead. It is a lot of fun to watch your project develop and very rewarding to see the finished design. These plates and glasses are available at any craft store. The white china plate makes a beautiful frame around the small salad plate when placed together. I always plan my design so that each plate complements the other for an effective presentation.

## Paint = Liquitex Glossies

Red

Maroon

Black

Pine Green

Yellow

Yellow Orange

Blue Purple

Gold

White

Maroon + Red (3:1)

Pine Green + touch of Maroon

Pine Green + Blue Purple (3:1)

## Materials

### ROYAL BRUSHES

▷ Series 5005, no. 10 Langnickel sable

▷ Series 599, nos. 2/0 and 5/0 White Taklon liners

▷ Series 179, nos. 2, 6 and 8 White Taklon cats tongue (filbert)

▷ Series 159, nos. 2, 4 and 8 White Taklon flat

### LEFRANC & BOURGEOIS BRUSHES

▷ Glass & Tile Brush, no. 8 flat, natural hair

### ADDITIONAL SUPPLIES

▷ toothpicks

▷ permanent fine-point pen

▷ rubbing alcohol

▷ lint-free paper towels

### SURFACE

▷ Glass and white china plates from any home decor or craft supply store.

This pattern may be hand-traced or photocopied for personal use only. Enlarge at 118% to bring it up to full size. It is used in this project on the large white plate.

These patterns may be hand-traced or photocopied for personal use only. Enlarge them at 154%. The pattern above is used on the clear glass plate. The pattern at right at is used on the clear drinking glass.

# Daisies

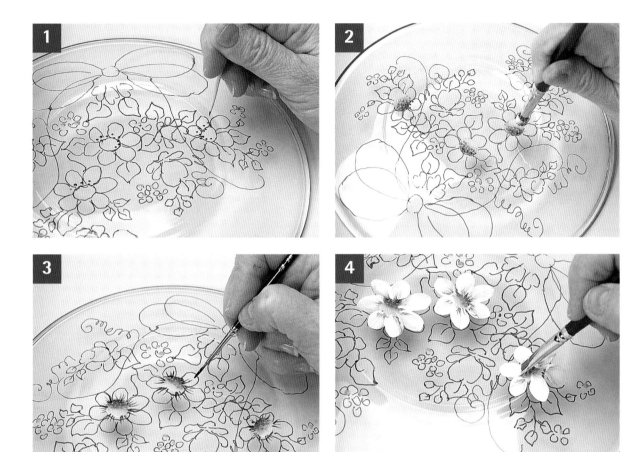

**1** Prepare the surface and trace the pattern onto the top of the plate using a permanent pen. You will be painting on the back of the plate, as this project uses the reverse painting technique (see page 23).

Painting on the back, use your pointed toothpick and with Black, place dots on the daisy centers. With Yellow Orange and a dulled toothpick, dot in the centers of the small flowers. Dry thoroughly.

**2** Double load your no. 10 sable with Yellow and a touch of White on one side and Maroon on the other. Both colors should be visible when you dab the brush on the palette. Dab in the center of the daisies, keeping the Maroon side of the brush over the previously placed Black dots. The center should definitely be dark on one side and light on the other. Turn the plate over and make sure that both colors are showing through. The yellow part should be away from the Black dots. Reload the brush if needed to complete the three daisy centers.

**3** Paint three very tiny veins on each daisy petal using your no. 2/0 liner brush and thinned Black (don't thin too much). Let dry.

**4** Load your no. 6 filbert with White, then add a touch of Gold on the side of the brush. The Gold is just a tint and should be very light. Pull one-stroke petals into the centers. It's okay for the paint to come into the center, but the petals do get narrower, so lift up the brush. The glass should show through the paint. Sometimes the Gold will show through, other times it won't. Be careful that the Gold is not always on the same side on each petal, or your flower will look too much like a pinwheel.

# Roses

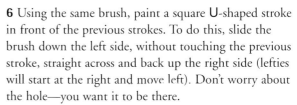

**5** Mix Maroon with a little Red (3:1) to brighten up the Maroon. Load your no. 8 flat into the mixture; then tip the corner of the brush in White. Paint two **U**-shaped strokes at the back of the center of a large rose, keeping the White side up. Place these two petals as close as you can to each other without touching. When painting in reverse, no stroke can overlap another.

**6** Using the same brush, paint a square **U**-shaped stroke in front of the previous strokes. To do this, slide the brush down the left side, without touching the previous stroke, straight across and back up the right side (lefties will start at the right and move left). Don't worry about the hole—you want it to be there.

**7** Next, to paint the two side petals, use the same brush, and press and slide the brush down each side, keeping the White toward the top. Be careful not to touch the previous strokes. For the rest of the roses, always paint the two side petals before moving on to the lower petals.

**8** Tucked right underneath the side petals are the second set of petals. Press and slide these in without touching the petals above.

# Roses continued

**9** With the chisel edge of your no. 8 flat, press down and pull the last petal at the bottom of the rose. Still be careful not to touch the above petals.

**10** Now dab straight Maroon into the opening with the corner of any brush that's comfortable for you. You don't have to be particular; the only part that will show from the front is what you filled in.

For the smaller rose, change to your no. 4 flat and paint it the same way you did the larger rose.

# Stems and Small Flowers

**11** Mix Pine Green a touch of Maroon to darken the Pine Green. Using your 5/0 liner, paint in all of the leaf stems. Allow to dry.

**12** Using your no. 2 flat and Blue Purple tipped in White, paint blossom strokes for the small flowers. Be careful not to overlap the petals. Notice that when you turn your plate over and look at the front, the flowers will probably look more blue than from the back. This is fine.

# Leaves and Ribbons

**13** Mix Pine Green and Blue Purple (3:1). Load your no. 8 filbert with this mix, tip in White, then blend on your palette. Paint one-stroke leaves, trying to keep the vein as the center of the leaf. Take care not to overlap the leaves, but it doesn't matter if you overlap a flower petal—it won't show from the front.

**14** Paint the smaller leaves toward the center of the design using your no. 2 filbert with the same colors and the same stroke as in step 13. To create the smaller leaves, don't press as hard as you did for the larger leaves. Leave some of the leaves around the edge of the design unpainted.

**15** Using your no. 2 filbert and Gold, paint in the small leaves at the outside of the design. The Gold is very transparent and will not appear to have covered. Let it dry; then check it again to see if it is dark enough. It is very pretty painted on thin with the light

shining through, but if you want it more solid, you can give the leaves another coat. Dry all paint thoroughly before proceeding.

To paint the ribbon, use your no. 8 Glass and Tile brush. Double load with Blue Purple and tip White on the edge; blend on the palette. Start with your brush on its tip at the beginning of the loop; then press down as you get to the middle and lift again as you get to the other end of the loop. Using the ribbon stroke, follow the ties in the same manner. Let dry; then determine if the ribbon needs a second coat. (See page 16 for specific ribbon directions.)

Mix Pine Green and Blue Purple (3:1) to make a very dark green mix. With this mix on your 2/0 liner, follow the pattern for your curlicues.

**16** With your dulled toothpick and White, add your final dip-dots, scattering them throughout.

# Finishing

**17** Once the paint has thoroughly dried, remove the pen and ink pattern from the front of the plate with rubbing alchohol and a lint-free paper towel. Bake your plate, paint side up, according to the paint manufacturer's instructions.

# Other Pieces

**18** Paint the front rim of the large white plate using the same colors you used for the blue flowers and ribbon on the glass plate. Begin with the ribbon as the first step. Paint the leaves using your no. 2 filbert with Pine Green double loaded with White. Finally, use your dulled toothpick and White paint to scatter dip-dots throughout.

Paint the outside of the drinking glass with the regular technique. Follow the same instructions as for the clear plate, but start with the ribbon as the first step. Paint the rest of the design in any order—flowers, leaves, filler flowers—ending with curlicues and highlights and dots.

# *Rooster*
# Set

Roosters are one of my favorite things to paint. I am so happy that they are such a popular decorating theme. We raise banty roosters, and I used them as a sample for this design. I am amazed at the beautiful colors that each one exhibits and by how much fun they are to watch as they go about their day.

I hope these designs will brighten your kitchen and be fun for you to paint.

## Paint = Liquitex Glossies

Red

Maroon

Blue

Pine Green

Yellow Orange

Black

White

Red + Maroon (3:1)

Blue + Red (6:1)

Pine Green + touch of blue/red mix

Pine Green + White (3:1)

## Materials

### ROYAL BRUSHES

- Series 159, no. 4 White Taklon flat

- Series 599, no. 5/0 White Taklon liner

- Series 179, no. 4 White Taklon cats tongue (filbert)

- Series 225, no. 3 sable round

- Series 5005, no. 8 Langnickel sable

### LEFRANC & BOURGEOIS BRUSHES

- Glass & Tile Brush, no. 8 flat, natural-hair

### ADDITIONAL SUPPLIES

- wax-free transfer paper

- ballpoint pen or stylus

- toothpicks

- rubbing alcohol

- lint-free paper towels

### SURFACE

- White 8-inch (20cm) tiles from any craft store or tile manufacturer.

This pattern may be hand-traced or photo-copied for personal use only. Enlarge at 133% to bring it up to full size.

# Rooster

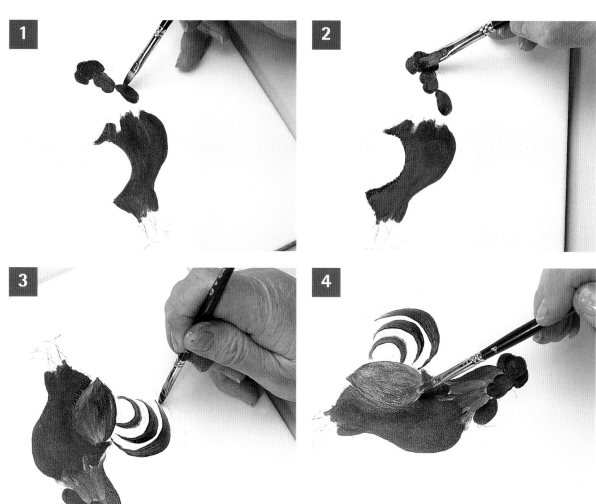

**1** Clean the tile with rubbing alcohol and a lint-free paper towel. Trace on the pattern. Mix a country red color using Red and Maroon (3:1). Use this mix and your no. 4 filbert to base in just the rooster breast and body (not the wings). Also base in the comb, the wattle and the red part of his face. If the red looks too streaky apply a second coat. Dry thoroughly.

**2** Load your no. 8 flat with the country red mixture, then side load with Blue. Shade next to the wing, keeping the Blue side near the wing. Also darken each side of the comb, the wattle next to the rooster, right below the neck feathers, between the legs, and the back edge of the face. Dry thoroughly.

**3** Mix Blue and the country red mix (6:1) to make a dark muted blue. Using your no. 4 filbert and this mixture, paint in the head and neck feathers and the wing. Add some blue tail feathers with a stroke similar to a ribbon stroke—start on the chisel edge, drag while pushing down; then allow the brush to return to a chisel edge as you reach the end of the feather. I find it easier to start at the body and stroke outward to make each feather. Dry thoroughly.

**4** Still using your no. 4 filbert, skim a little Pine Green and White (3:1) over the wing.

# Feathers

**5** With your no. 4 filbert, streak a little red mixture onto the wing. Then come back over it with just a light touch of White.

**6** Mix Pine Green and a touch of the dark blue mix and paint in more tail feathers with your no. 4 filbert using the ribbon stroke. If you would like to add variation to the feathers, slide one side of your brush into White. Keep the green mixture on your brush and side load a little White to pull feathers from the neck up into the head.

**7** With your no. 4 filbert, add tail feathers using the red mixture and the ribbon stroke. You can add a little White to your red tail feathers if you want to tone them down a bit. You can also add more blue or green feathers if you would like. Let each color dry before applying another feather color.

Double load your no. 4 filbert with red mix and a bit of White. Highlight the comb, the wattle and the face, keeping the highlight on the outside edge. Refer to the photo for highlight placement.

Lightly outline the comb, face, wattle, chest and wing with Black using your liner brush.

**8** With your no. 5/0 liner and Black, paint little loops on your rooster's chest and wing. Also add the Black dot for the rooster's eye; then touch on a little White highlight. For each chest loop, add a little White dot using a pointed toothpick; place a few on the wing as well. Dry thoroughly.

# Final Steps

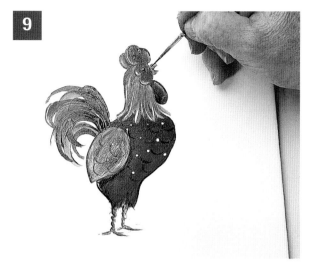

**9** With Orange and your liner brush, basecoat the feet and the beak. Outline the back of the legs with Black using short choppy strokes. Outline under the feet also. Outline the beak in Black; then add a touch of White for highlighting. Highlight the face, then highlight the front of the legs using the same short choppy strokes as were used on the back.

**10** With a scant amount of Pine Green on your no. 8 Langnickel, lightly dab on the grass. Place some above the feet so the rooster appears to be set into the grass. With your liner, pull up grass blades in curved strokes. Add three or four White dot flowers with your dulled toothpick; then dot in Orange centers. You can add some Pine Green leaves with the toothpick if you like.

Finish with strokework around the edges using your no. 3 round and your dark blue mix. The lines on the pattern on page 96 are center guidelines for the comma strokes.

**11** Bake your tile according to the paint manufacturer's instructions.

# *Casserole* Dishes

I t is so fun to take your handpainted casserole dishes to pot-luck lunches and covered-dish dinners. You'll surely be able to quickly reclaim your dish, as it is so easy to recognize. It's also a great way to advertise your business if you paint to sell.

I purchased these casserole dishes at a local discount variety store. You can adapt the patterns to any size dish that you choose.

## Paint = Liquitex Glossies

Blue Purple

Blue

Aqua

Bright Blue

Pine Green

Yellow

Orange

Brown

White

Black

Blue + White (3:1)

Orange + Red (1:1)

Blue + Blue Purple
(1:1)

## Materials

### ROYAL BRUSHES

▶ Series 179, nos. 2, 4, 6 and 8
White Taklon cats tongue (filbert)

▶ Series 159, nos. 4, 6 and 8
White Taklon flat

▶ Series 158, no. 5/0 White Taklon script

▶ Series 599, no. 5/0 White Taklon liner

▶ Series 5005, no. 8 Langnickel sable

### ADDITIONAL SUPPLIES

▶ toothpick

▶ wax-free transfer paper

▶ ballpoint pen or stylus

▶ rubbing alcohol

▶ Q-tip

▶ lint-free paper towels

▶ sponge

### SURFACE

▶ Clear casserole dishes from
any craft supply or variety store.

These patterns may be hand-traced or photocopied
for personal use only. The top pattern, for the large
dish, appears here at full size.

    Enlarge the bottom pattern, for the small dish, at
130% to bring it up to full size.

# Large Dish

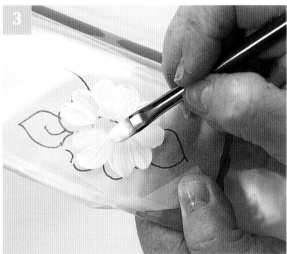

**1** Attach the pattern inside of the casserole dish as you did the glass salad bowl (page 33). To paint the blue flowers, you will layer three values of blue: Aqua, Blue and Blue Purple. First load your 5/0 script liner with Blue Purple and begin the stroke near the center of the flower, then pull out. Continue this all the way around each blue flower. Dry thoroughly.

Mix Blue and White (3:1), and sporadically apply this color using the same brush and the same stroke. You don't want to cover the first color completely, so skip around. Dry thoroughly.

For the third blue, load the brush with Aqua, then slide one side of the brush into White to double load your brush. The Aqua should be the dominant color on the brush with the White serving as an accent. Streak this in, filling in a bit more in the upper left-hand corner of the blue flowers. Stop just before you think it's enough. Add some White here and there to accent.

**2** Using your no. 8 Langnickel, tap in the flower centers using Yellow double loaded with Orange as we have done before. Touch into White and dab into the upper center of the flower center. Add Black and White dots with toothpicks to finish the flower.

**3** For the dogwood flowers, basecoat a heart shape with two strokes per petal using White on your no. 8 filbert. Leave a dip in the top. For solid coverage, you will need two coats; however, I do not mind some transparency, as the glass showing through gives a shaded effect.

**4** Darken next to the center with Brown on your no. 8 flat. Also float a concave stroke around the dips at the end of the petals.

# Flower Centers and Vine

**5** Fill in the centers of the dogwood flowers exactly like you did the blue flowers. With your 5/0 script liner, make a mixture of Brown with a little Black. Paint the little lines coming out of the center of the flower.

**6** Outline your flower with Brown. With your dulled toothpick, dot in Black on the ends of the lines and dot in Black and White around the center.

**7** Connect the flowers with a winding vine using Pine Green and your 5/0 liner. Add the leaf stems as well.

**8** Double load your no. 6 filbert with Pine Green and White and paint the large leaves with one or two strokes. Make small one-stroke leaves with your no. 4 filbert. Add White dots with your dulled toothpick.

**9** Dampen the sponge (any type will do); then squeeze the moisture out with a paper towel. Dip the sponge in one of the blue mixtures used for the blue flower, then tap on the palette to distribute. Sponge this on just the top edge of the bowl. Alternate with the other blues used in the project, and add a light touch of White for variety. If you need to clean up the edges, use your Q-tip barely moistened with rubbing alcohol.

# Small Dish

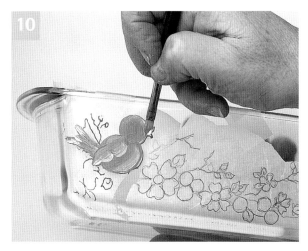

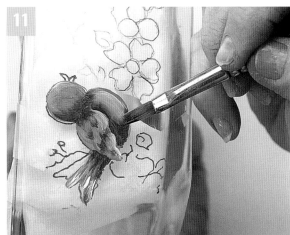

**10** To paint the small casserole dish, use Bright Blue and your no. 4 filbert to base in the body and head of the bird. Use the chisel edge of your brush to establish a pattern of tail feathers. Dry thoroughly and apply a second coat in the same fashion.

   Double load your brush with Bright Blue and White and highlight the strategic areas: right on the edge of the wing, the breast, and the head. Pull a little into the tail. This sets up the shape of the little bird.

**11** Shade by floating Blue Purple, loaded on your no. 6 flat, on the back of the head, then blend it out around the base of the head. From the head, shade down onto the upper body of the bird to connect the head to the body. Slide the brush using short strokes on the wing just to establish the sections of the wing. Shade under the wing, then walk the color toward the front of the bird.

**12** Using your no. 4 flat and a mix of Aqua and White (1:1), highlight the wings. Use little C-strokes and pull the feathers of the wings out. Highlight the breast and the tips of the tail.

**13** Mix Orange and Red (1:1) with your no. 8 Lang-nickel, then side load with a little White. Dab the brush on a paper towel to remove the excess paint. Dab on the cheek with a light tap, keeping the White toward the top of the cheek. Drybrush a tint onto the breast area using the same mixture and brush.

   With your 5/0 liner, dot in a Black eye and add tiny strokes around the eye. Add a dot of White in the upper right corner of the eye for a highlight.

# Bird and Berries

**14** Still using your liner brush, paint the beak with Orange. Add just a touch of White to highlight the beak, then add some dots on the chest; also add the tree limbs with Brown.

**15** Mix Blue and Blue Purple (1:1) and basecoat the blueberries with two coats of paint using your no. 2 filbert brush. Dry thoroughly.

**16** Mix Aqua and White (1:1). With your no. 2 filbert, float this mixture around the bottom of each berry and a little on the top of each berry to make it appear round.

Now touch a tiny bit of highlight on each berry with White and your liner brush.

**17** Paint the dogwood flowers, leaves and the top edge using the same colors you used for the large casserole. Use smaller sizes of filbert brushes.

**18** Bake the casserole dishes according to your paint manufacturer's instructions.

# *Stained Glass*
# Bottle

I used Lefranc & Bourgeois Glass & Tile paints for this project because they are made to be transparent, and they offer a beautiful stained glass look. Although the colors are transparent, they have a vivacious and brilliant effect.

On this project only I used a pure red sable brush because I could flatten it out wide and pull it up to a skinny point to make a good flower shape.

## Paint = Lefranc & Bourgeois

Purple

Lapis Lazuli

Cypress Green

Amethyst Violet

Poppy Red

Tropical Yellow

## Materials

### ROYAL BRUSHES

▷ Series 1250, no. 5 pure red sable

### LEFRANC & BOURGEOIS BRUSHES

▷ Glass & Tile brush, no. 8 flat, natural-hair

### ADDITIONAL SUPPLIES

▷ Lefranc & Bourgeois Glass & Tile Colors Gold Outliner

▷ Lefranc & Bourgeois Glass, Tile and Metal Works Retarder/Thinning Medium

▷ rubbing alcohol

▷ lint-free paper towels

▷ all purpose hobby glue

▷ cork—usually the bottles you buy have fitting corks, but these can be purchased separately at craft and hobby stores

▷ marble—transparent colors are best and can be bought in a small mesh bag (inexpensive) at craft and hobby stores

▷ paring knife or scissors

### SURFACE

▷ Any size clear decorative bottle found at hobby, craft or home goods stores.

# Iris

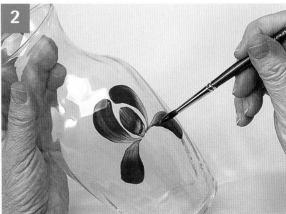

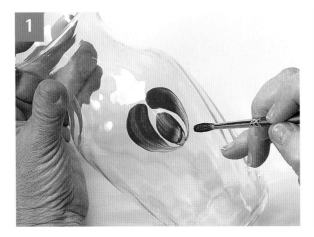

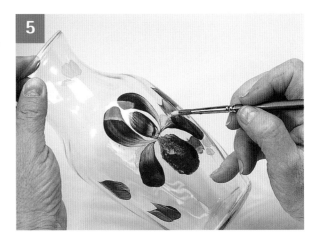

**1** Prepare the surface. I am using an inexpensive, clear glass vase for this project. No pattern is needed. With Purple on your no. 5 sable, make a center press-pull stroke two-thirds of the way up the surface. Make the stroke wider at the top than at the bottom. To each side of this stroke make large comma strokes.

**2** Make two more comma strokes for the bottom petals of the iris. You can turn the vase upside down for these strokes if it is easier for you.

**3** Turn the vase upside down and pull the bottom center stroke by pressing down firmly on the glass. Then jiggle and release.

**4** If you want some buds on your vase, apply two comma strokes next to each other as shown. Rinse your brush and blot well.

**5** With the same brush, dab Tropical Yellow onto the tops of the bottom layer of petals.

# Blossoms, Buds and Outlining

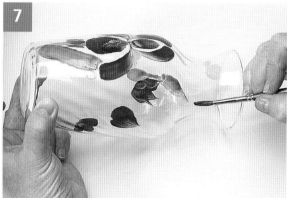

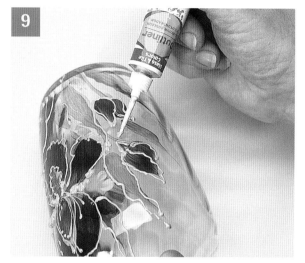

**6** Use Lapis Lazuli to paint in some freehand blossoms. I made iris buds by pressing hard and then pulling to a point. Keep this short and not too thin. You can make almost any kind of shape and outline it anywhere you have a flower.

**7** With Cypress Green on either your no. 5 sable or your no. 8 Glass & Tile brush, make a long ribbon stroke leaf by beginning at the bottom and pulling up. Stop at the bottom of the flower and finish above the flower with a tiny point. You can twist your brush a little to make it look like the leaf has turned. Keep adding greenery until you are satisfied. Don't worry about imperfections; you will cover them up with the gold liner pen. Using your no. 8 Glass & Tile brush, add Tropical Yellow daisy strokes into spaces that appear to need filling.

**8** Practice outlining with the gold outliner on a piece of paper before you try this on your vase. The harder you press, the fatter the line. When you're ready, outline the elements on the vase, but don't try to be too precise. Don't follow the lines of your flowers exactly; keep the

lines kind of jiggly and fun. Those of you who have done fabric painting will be good at this. Once you get started, you're going to use this little liner all the time.

**9** Continue adding the outlines. Turn your vase as needed to help with the application. You may prefer a black outline as shown on page 113; this is applied in the same way as the gold outliner.

---

## Hint

If your outliner keeps running when you want it to stop, just push very gently on the sides of the tube and it usually stops the flow by sucking a little air back into the tube.

# Tulip Bottle

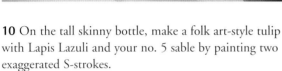

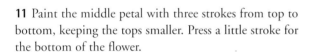

**10** On the tall skinny bottle, make a folk art-style tulip with Lapis Lazuli and your no. 5 sable by painting two exaggerated S-strokes.

**11** Paint the middle petal with three strokes from top to bottom, keeping the tops smaller. Press a little stroke for the bottom of the flower.

**12** Add some little rose circles of Lapis Lazuli, Purple or Poppy Red (I used all three colors). Or use Amethyst Violet or whatever color you would like. Make sure to place some on the neck to keep if from looking too boring. You already know how to make an iris, so place them wherever you like.

*Note: If you use a dirty brush (without rinsing), you will get an attractive variation in your colors.*

**13** Add a little thinning medium to the Cypress Green to make the color a little lighter and to help move the paint easier on the glass. With either brush, paint in the tulip leaves just like the iris leaves. Paint the filler leaf strokes with just a little push, then pull to a point.

**14** Outline the element with the gold outliner in the same way as you did for the vase. To outline the roses, start with a little half-circle around the top for a bowl. Then make marks to show the petals. Vary the position of the roses so they aren't all facing in the same direction. Keep it free and fun, and don't be too particular.

# Cork Top

**15** Add a little embellishment to the cork top. Carve out a little hole in the top of the cork using a paring knife or scissors, whichever you are comfortable with. Be careful!

**16** Glue the marble, jewel or whatever you have available to the top of the cork with a strong craft glue made for attaching different surfaces.

**17** Bake the vases and bottle according to the paint manufacturer's instructions.

PROJECT 15

*Little Pig*

# Tile

T he simplicity of this little pig just adds to his charm. I painted him in response to the many requests that I get from my friends and customers who collect pigs.

## Materials

### ROYAL BRUSHES

▷ Series 159, no. 8 White Taklon flat

▷ Series 5005, no. 8 Langnickel sable

▷ Series 599, no. 5/0 White Taklon liner

▷ Series 225, no. 1 sable round

### ADDITIONAL SUPPLIES

▷ wax-free transfer paper

▷ ballpoint pen or stylus

▷ rubbing alcohol

▷ toothpick

▷ paper towels

### SURFACE

▷ 4-inch (10cm) square white tiles from any craft supply or tile store.

## Paint = Liquitex Glossies

Almond

Brown

Red

Black

Pine Green

Maroon

Blue

White

Blue + Maroon (3:1)

Maroon + Red (1:1)

Red + White (1:1)

These patterns may be hand-traced or photocopied for personal use only. They appear here at full size.

**1** Transfer the pattern onto the surface with transfer paper and a stylus. With your no. 8 flat, basecoat the pig with Almond. You may need two coats. Allow to dry completely. With the same brush, double load Almond and Brown to shade. It's okay if this looks a little rough—it's pig skin.

**2** Using your no. 8 sable, drybrush in a few Brown spots. Don't use too much paint, as it should be a dry-brushed look. With the color still on your brush, rub a little on the pig in different places to muddy it up just a bit.

**3** Add some Red and White to the same brush. Blot this on your paper towel; then dab onto the cheeks for a very light blush. Also dab a little on the pig's behind.

# Finishing

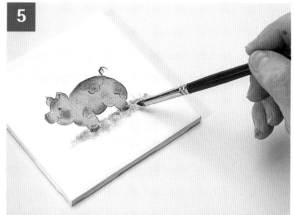

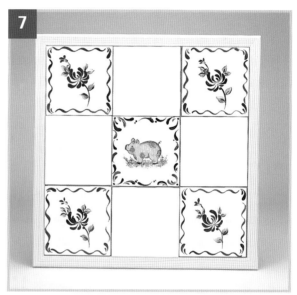

**4** Outline and detail the pig as shown with Brown on your 5/0 liner. Using Brown plus a bit of Black, darken the hooves and paint in the eye and tail. Dot a bit of White in the eye and on the cheek for the highlight.

**5** Still using your no. 8 sable, dab in Pine Green around the pig's feet. To darken the grass in some areas, add a tiny bit of Red to it.

**6** Pull up a few strands of grass with the darker green mix and the liner. Paint leaves with the same mix and a dulled toothpick. Fill in with White and Blue flowers using the dip-dot technique. Add a comma stroke border to frame your little pig.

**7** Paint the flowers with comma strokes using your no. 1 round (see page 16). Mix Blue and Maroon (3:1) for the blue flowers. Mix Maroon and Blue (1:1) for the red flowers. Make one-stroke leaves using a brush loaded with Pine Green and tipped in White. Paint the decoration on the outside of the tile with a ribbon stroke using a contrasting color. For example, if the flower is blue, use the red mix for the ribbon.

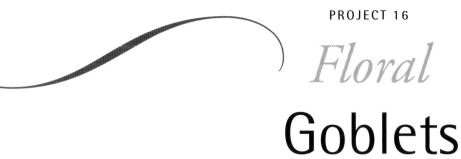

# *Floral*
# Goblets

I painted these goblets using various strokes. Practice doing each stroke on a practice piece to get the flow of the paint on glass. If you can perfect your strokework, you will not believe how quickly this project can be accomplished.

It is easy to find these water goblets. I purchased them at Garden Ridge Pottery but have seen them at almost every store that carries glassware.

Yellow is a very transparent color, so I always mix it with a touch of White to make it more opaque (6:1). There should be no visible color change in the Yellow, but it will be more opaque.

## Materials

### ROYAL BRUSHES

▶ Series 599, no. 5/0 White Taklon liner

▶ Series 159, no. 6 or 8 White Taklon flat

▶ Series 5005, no. 8 Langnickel sable

▶ Series 179, nos. 4 and 6 White Taklon cats tongue (filbert)

### ADDITIONAL SUPPLIES

▶ ballpoint pen or stylus

▶ rubbing alcohol

▶ Scotch Magic Tape

▶ lint-free paper towels

▶ toothpicks

### SURFACE

▶ Glass stemware from craft, hobby, or any store that carries glassware.

## Paint = Liquitex Glossies

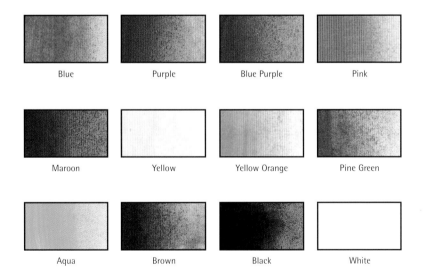

| | | | |
|---|---|---|---|
| Blue | Purple | Blue Purple | Pink |
| Maroon | Yellow | Yellow Orange | Pine Green |
| Aqua | Brown | Black | White |

◄ Yellow Blossoms

Blue Blossoms ▼

Purple Blossoms ▼

Pink Blossoms ▼

These patterns may be hand-traced or photocopied for personal use only. Enlarge at 133% to bring them up to full size.

# Pink Flowers

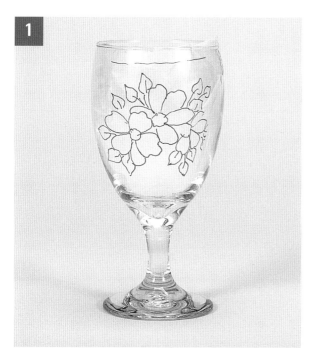

**1** Clean the surface and prepare using rubbing alcohol and a lint-free paper towel. Tape the pattern to the inside of the glass. Draw a line at the top about ½-inch (1.2cm) below the rim of the glass to align the pattern. Place wadded paper towels inside the glass to press the pattern closer to the surface (refer to page 19).

**2** Load your no. 6 filbert with Pink and tip the brush into White. Blend on your palette once or twice. Stroke in the flower petals from the outside of the petal, pulling in to the center. Some petals will take two strokes; some will take three strokes. Reload the brush every two strokes to get good color variation. Dry thoroughly.

**3** With your no. 6 or 8 flat, float Maroon next to the center of the flower with the clean part of the brush pointing toward the outside edge of the petal. Use a zig-zag motion, keeping the brush pressed against the glass.

**4** Mix Yellow with a small touch of Maroon to make a nice rich brown. First, tap the Yellow into the center of the flower with your no. 8 Langnickel. Then side load the same brush with the brown mixture. Tap on your palette to distribute the paint and dab the brush onto the flower center, keeping the brown toward the bottom. Add a dab of White toward the center top.

# Leaves and Yellow Flowers

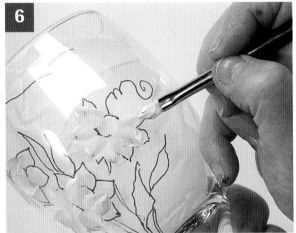

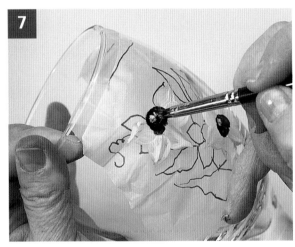

**5** With a dulled toothpick, dot in some Black around the flower center. Paint the one-stroke leaves using your no. 4 filbert and a mixture of Pine Green and Maroon (9:1), double loaded with White. Add curlicues using your no. 5/0 liner and the green mix (thinned). Dot in White using a dulled toothpick.

**6** For the yellow flowers, mix Yellow and White (6:1) for the yellow mix. Load your no. 6 filbert with the yellow mix; then triple load by touching one side in White and one in Yellow Orange. Keep yellow as your most dominant color. Paint the petals using a leaf stroke, starting at the center of the flower and stroking outward leaving a pointed tip. Flip the brush now and then so the color will vary on each petal.

**7** Pounce in the centers with Brown on your no. 8 Langnickel. When dry, tap in a dab of White for highlighting.

**8** Paint the leaves with your no. 8 flat brush using Pine Green mixed with a touch of Brown side loaded with White. For the longer leaves, start on the chisel edge of your brush and press and wiggle the brush slightly as you move toward the point on the end. Press and lift the brush to make smaller one-stroke leaves. Use the chisel edge of your brush to paint in the stem.

# Blue Flowers

**9** Finish the goblet with curlicues and White dots as stated in step 5.

**10** To paint the morning glories, make the following three mixtures:
*Mix no. 1*—Blue and Purple (3:1).
*Mix no. 2*—White and Mix no.1 (9:1) to make a light blue value.
*Mix no. 3*—Aqua and White (1:1)

Load your no. 6 flat with mix no. 2; then dip one side in mix no. 1 and the other side in White (you will have a triple-loaded brush). Blend this mixture on the palette. It's important to have a nice White edge on one side, as well as a nice dark blue edge on the other side. Practice loading your brush to achieve good, crisp color changes. Alternate the light edge of the petal by randomly side loading into mix no. 3 instead of White. This gives an added tint to the lightest part of the petal.

Paint each petal with a double-leaf stroke, keeping the White on the outside edge of both strokes. Paint the trumpet part of the blue flower with mix no. 1.

**11** With your no. 8 Langnickel, tap mix no. 1 into the center of the blue flower. Make this fade into the dark edge of each petal.

# Leaves and Purple Flowers

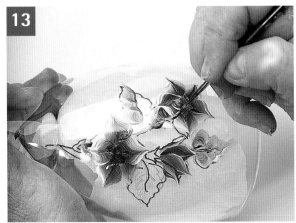

**12** For the blue flower leaves, mix Pine Green with a tiny bit of mix no. 1 to darken. Load this mix onto your no. 6 flat, then side load with White and blend on your palette. Keep the White toward the outside edge. Beginning at the large end of the leaf, paint little C-strokes coming up to the point as shown.

**13** With the same green mixture, paint the calyx. Use your liner brush with Yellow Orange and Yellow to dab in the centers of the flowers. Finish with the curlicues and dots as shown in step 5.

**14** To begin the purple flower goblet, establish the dark part of the back petal by floating a mix of Blue Purple and Purple (4:1) and very little water or medium. Use your no. 8 flat and paint the wiggle float as described on page 15. Float this mix only on the back petals of the blossom. Allow to dry.

**15** With the same purple mix and White double loaded on your no. 8 flat, press down and paint a lacy-edged blossom stroke, keeping the White to the outside edge. The dark part of the brush should meet with the previous float, and this will fill in the whole petal. Paint all the back petals.

# Purple Flowers continued

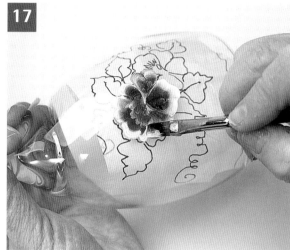

**16** Double load your no. 8 flat with Purple and White. Keep the White on the outside edge and paint in the large front petal. Keep the edge of the petal ruffled. There will be an unpainted area in the center of the flower, but that's okay.

**17** Wipe off the brush so the White isn't on the edge and pick up Purple. Fill in the rest of the petal with that same flowing stroke. You can fill in any unpainted area with Purple if you need to.

**18** Use your no. 5/0 liner and Black to fill in the little lines that go around the petals. If you want to clean these petals up a bit, outline lightly between them. If your Black strokes don't show up enough, touch them up with a tiny bit of White.

**19** Mix Yellow and White (1:1) and use your no. 5/0 liner to add the seeds with little press-and-lift strokes. Right inside of each seed add a little Orange highlight. Outline one side of each seed with a tiny bit of White.

# Finishing

**20** Mix Pine Green with a touch of Purple to darken. Use your no. 6 flat to paint the leaves the same as you did the blue flower leaves. Finish with curlicues and White dots.

**21** Bake your goblets according to the paint manufacturer's instructions.

# Resources

A Couple of Ideas
5102 S. 65th West Avenue
Tulsa, OK 74107
Phone: (918) 446-8625
CarolOkie@aol.com

Apple Barrel Gloss Paint
Plaid Enterprises, Inc.
Norcross GA 30091-7600
www.plaidonline.com

DecoArt Inc.
Stanford, KY 40494
www.decoart.com

Delta Perm Enamel
Delta Technical Coatings, Inc
Whittier, CA 90601

Liquitex Glossies Paint and
Lefranc & Bourgeois
Glass & Tile Paint and Brushes
ColArt Americas, Inc.
11 Constitution Avenue
P.O. Box 1396
Piscataway, NJ 08855-1396
*Note: Both Liquitex and Lefranc
Bourgeois are owned by ColArt*

## RETAILERS IN CANADA

Crafts Canada
2745 Twenty-ninth St. NE
Calgary, Alberta T1Y 7B5

Folk Art Enterprises
P.O. Box 1088
Ridgetown, Ontario N0P 2C0
Phone: (888) 214-0062

MacPherson Craft Wholesale
83 Queen St. E.
P.O. Box 1870
St. Mary's, Ontario N4X 1C2
Phone: (519) 284-1741

Maureen McNaughton Enterprises
RR #2
Belwood, Ontario N0B 1J0
Phone: (519) 843-5648

Mercury Art & Craft Supershop
332 Wellington St.
London, Ontario N6C 4P7
Phone: (519) 434-1636

Town & Country Folk Art Supplies
93 Green Lane
Thornhill, Ontario L3T 6K6
Phone: (905) 882-0199

## RETAILERS IN UNITED KINGDOM

Art Express
Index House
70 Burley Road
Leeds LS3 1JX
Tel: 0800 731 4185
www.artexpress.co.uk

Crafts World (head office only)
No 8 North Street, Guildford
Surrey GU1 4AF
Tel: 07000 757070
Telephone for local store

Chroma Colour Products
Unit 5 Pilton Estate
Pitlake
Croydon CR0 3RA
Tel: 020 8688 1991
www.chromacolour.com

Green & Stone
259 King's Road
London SW3 5EL
Tel: 020 7352 0837
greenandstone@enterprise.net

Hobbycrafts (head office only)
River Court
Southern Sector
Bournemouth International Airport
Christchurch
Dorset BH23 6SE
Tel: 0800 272387 freephone
Telephone for local store

Homecrafts Direct
P.O. Box 38
Leicester LE1 9BU
Tel: 0116 251 3139
Mail order service

# Index